Eyewitness
FOSSIL

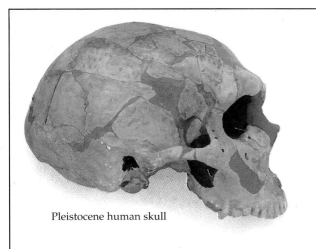

Pleistocene human skull

Eocene gastropods

Eocene fish

Triassic swimming reptile

Cretaceous dinosaur
finger bones

Jurassic brittlestar

Cretaceous
cone (sectioned
and polished)

Cretaceous cone

Ordovician nautiloid
(polished and shaped)

Jurassic sea urchin

Carboniferous
horsetail

Modern
horsetail

Eocene
shark
tooth

Pleistocene coral

Carboniferous
fern

Eyewitness
FOSSIL

Written by
DR. PAUL D. TAYLOR

Jurassic ammonite
(carved as a snakestone)

Triassic
dinosaur
footprint

Carboniferous
lycopod

Eocene fish

Silurian
brachiopod

Pleistocene
hand ax

Permian tree fern
(sectioned and polished)

Modern
coral

Pliocene scallop

Pleistocene
coral

DK Publishing, Inc.

Cretaceous
dinosaur tooth

Jurassic
ammonite

Carboniferous spider

Pleistocene sea urchin

Cretaceous
opalized
gastropod

Cretaceous
opalized bivalve

Cretaceous bryozoan

Cretaceous worm tube

Jurassic coral (sectioned
and polished)

Miocene corals

DK

LONDON, NEW YORK, MELBOURNE,
MUNICH, and DELHI

Project editor Louise Pritchard
Art editor Alison Anholt-White
Senior editor Sophie Mitchell
Senior art editor Julia Harris
Editorial director Sue Unstead
Art director Anne-Marie Bulat
Special photography Colin Keates
(Natural History Museum, London)

REVISED EDITION
Managing editors Linda Esposito, Andrew Macintyre
Managing art editor Jane Thomas
Category publisher Linda Martin
Art director Simon Webb
Editor and reference compiler Clare Hibbert
Art editor Joanna Pocock
Consultant Kim Bryan
Production Jenny Jacoby
Picture research Celia Dearing
DTP designer Siu Yin Ho

U.S. editor Elizabeth Hester
Senior editor Beth Sutinis
Art director Dirk Kaufman
U.S. production Chris Avgherinos
U.S. DTP designer Milos Orlovic

This Eyewitness ® Guide has been conceived by
Dorling Kindersley Limited and Editions Gallimard

This edition first published in the United States in 2004
by DK Publishing, Inc., 375 Hudson Street, New York, NY 10014

08 10 9 8 7 6 5

Copyright © 1990, © 2003, Dorling Kindersley Limited

A catalog record for this book is available from the Library of Congress.
ISBN 13: 978-0-7566-0682-4 (PLC)
ISBN-13: 978-0-7566-0681-7 (ALB)
Color reproduction by Colourscan, Singapore
Printed in China by Toppan Printing Co. (Shenzhen) Ltd.

Discover more at
www.dk.com

Pleistocene
gastropods

Silurian
sea lily

Miocene bat jaws

19th-century
microscope for
examining thin
sections

Slide of thin section of
Carboniferous bryozoans

Modern
magnolia flower

Contents

Jurassic
ammonites

Silurian trilobite
(mounted as a brooch)

Fossils-true and false

F OSSILS ARE THE REMAINS or evidence of animals or plants that have been preserved naturally. They range in size from huge dinosaur skeletons to tiny plants and animals which can only be seen under a microscope. Most fossils are formed from the hard parts of animals and plants, such as shells, bones, teeth, or wood. They may be virtually unchanged from the originals, or they may be mineral replacements. Animals and plants have also been preserved in peat, tar, ice, and amber, the resin of ancient trees. Eggs, footprints, and burrows can be fossilized too. The study of fossils, called paleontology, shows us that life originated on Earth at least 3,500 million years ago. Since then there has been a succession of animal and plant species. Most are now extinct, and only a tiny number have survived as fossils. By studying these survivors, we can get a fascinating glimpse of ancient life on Earth.

WHAT CAN IT BE?
Although people have been collecting fossils for hundreds of years, the true nature of them was a mystery until relatively recently. This illustration appeared in an Italian book published in 1670.

RARE DELICACY
Detailed fossils of plants are rare because they rot away quickly when they die. In this leaf, however, even the delicate veins have been preserved.

PEARLY AMMONITE
The mollusks known as ammonites (pp. 28-29) are now extinct. They had hard shells made of a chalky mineral called aragonite, with a colorful outer layer of mother-of-pearl. This one has been preserved almost in its original state.

ONLY BONES
Bones are often the only remains of animals because they are the hardest parts. This is the fossilized vertebra from the backbone of an ancient, giant swimming reptile called a plesiosaur (pp. 46–47).

Trilobite cast and mold

TAKING SHAPE
Fossils are often found in two parts. Sometimes, after burial, an animal rots away, and leaves a hollow mold. If the mold is then filled by sediment (p. 9) it may harden to form a cast.

Plesiosaur tooth

HARD TOOTH
Teeth are often found as fossils, as they are made of hard material.

PRECIOUS WOOD
One kind of fossilization occurs when chemical changes cause a mineral to grow, grain by grain, in place of the original tissues of the animal or plant. The tissues of this fossilized wood have been replaced by opal.

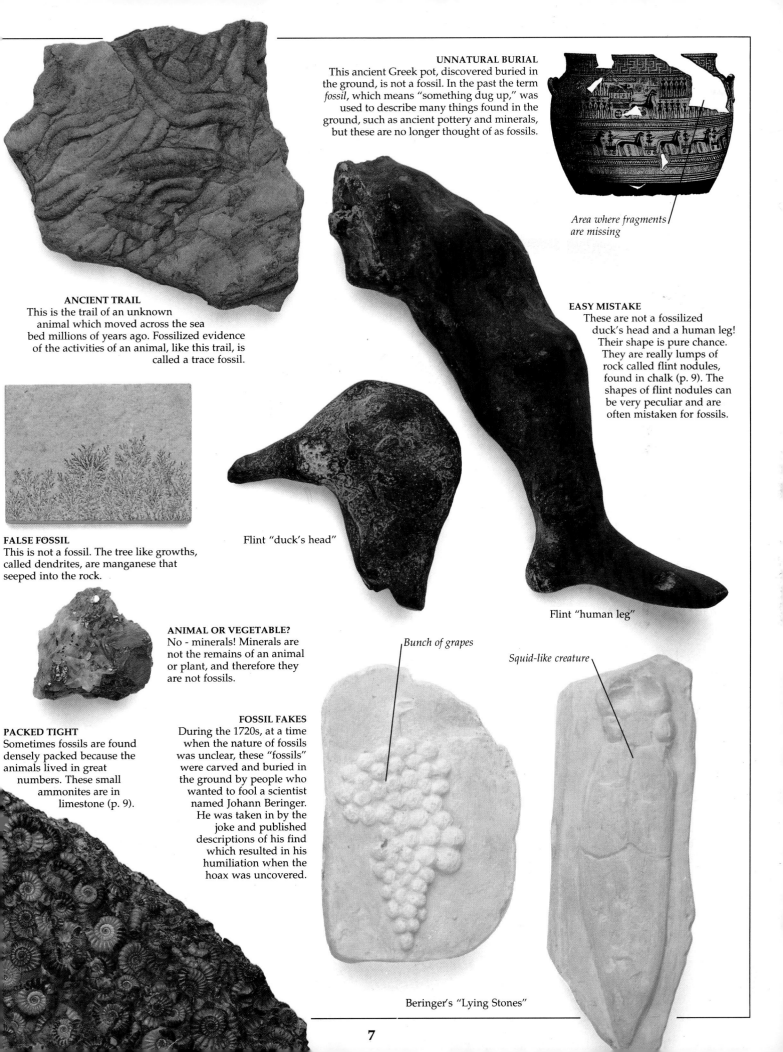

ANCIENT TRAIL
This is the trail of an unknown animal which moved across the sea bed millions of years ago. Fossilized evidence of the activities of an animal, like this trail, is called a trace fossil.

UNNATURAL BURIAL
This ancient Greek pot, discovered buried in the ground, is not a fossil. In the past the term *fossil*, which means "something dug up," was used to describe many things found in the ground, such as ancient pottery and minerals, but these are no longer thought of as fossils.

Area where fragments are missing

EASY MISTAKE
These are not a fossilized duck's head and a human leg! Their shape is pure chance. They are really lumps of rock called flint nodules, found in chalk (p. 9). The shapes of flint nodules can be very peculiar and are often mistaken for fossils.

Flint "duck's head"

Flint "human leg"

FALSE FOSSIL
This is not a fossil. The tree like growths, called dendrites, are manganese that seeped into the rock.

ANIMAL OR VEGETABLE?
No - minerals! Minerals are not the remains of an animal or plant, and therefore they are not fossils.

PACKED TIGHT
Sometimes fossils are found densely packed because the animals lived in great numbers. These small ammonites are in limestone (p. 9).

FOSSIL FAKES
During the 1720s, at a time when the nature of fossils was unclear, these "fossils" were carved and buried in the ground by people who wanted to fool a scientist named Johann Beringer. He was taken in by the joke and published descriptions of his find which resulted in his humiliation when the hoax was uncovered.

Bunch of grapes

Squid-like creature

Beringer's "Lying Stones"

The making of rocks

THE MANY KINDS OF ROCKS beneath our feet have been forming for more than 4,000 million years. The Earth's crust is made up of elements. The important ones are oxygen, silicon, aluminum, iron, calcium, sodium, potassium, magnesium, and carbon. These combine in different ways to form minerals. All rocks are made up of minerals. Common rock-forming minerals include calcite (calcium carbonate), quartz (silicon dioxide), and feldspars (complex minerals containing aluminum, silicon, calcium, sodium, and potassium). There are three groups of rocks: igneous, metamorphic, and sedimentary.

AMETHYST
This is the purple variety of the mineral quartz. If allowed to grow freely, quartz crystals are pointed and hexagonal (six-sided).

FOLDED ROCK
Powerful movements in the Earth's crust can cause rocks to crack and form faults, or to buckle, creating folds like this.

Distorted trilobite

TWISTED TRILOBITE
Metamorphic rocks may contain distorted fossils such as this trilobite (p. 30) in slate.

Feldspar *Mica* *Quartz*

Black mica
Glassy quartz
White feldspar

Thin section of granite

GRANITE
The speckles in this granite are individual minerals. Granite is an igneous rock formed at great depths.

Molten rocks

Igneous rocks are formed by the cooling of molten magma (liquid rock) from deep within the Earth. Sometimes the magma reaches the surface and erupts from volcanoes as lava before it cools. Most often, though, the magma cools and becomes solid deep underground.

LAYER UPON LAYER
The Grand Canyon in Arizona, formed by the erosion of sandstone and limestone, is a natural slice through the Earth's crust. The oldest stratum, or layer, is at the bottom, the youngest at the top.

Band rich in mica

Band rich in quartz

SCHIST
Parallel banding of minerals is a common feature of metamorphic rocks. Schist is formed from shale or mud.

Changed rocks

High temperatures and pressures can change rocks into new types called metamorphic rocks. Marble is a metamorphosed limestone; slate, a metamorphosed shale.

Band of quartz

Band of silicate minerals

Thin section of schist

One varve

Fine sediment
Coarse sediment

ROCK BANDS
Stratification on a much smaller scale than the Grand Canyon is seen in this sedimentary rock. Each set of one light layer (fine sediment) and one dark layer (coarse sediment) is a year's accumulation of silt and mud, called a varve, at the bottom of a glacier-fed lake. Such well-defined seasonal bands are rare.

CHALK CLIFFS
Chalk is a pure white limestone composed mostly of the skeletons of tiny marine plants.

CONGLOMERATE
This is a coarse sedimentary rock consisting of rounded pebbles bound together by a natural mineral cement. Conglomerate can look a lot like manufactured concrete.

Pebble

Natural cement

Loose sand grains

Sandstone

Quartz

Iron-rich cement

Thin section of sandstone

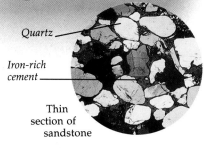

Deposited rocks

Rocks are continually being eroded, creating grains which are carried by rivers, by the sea, and by the wind. These grains are deposited, together with the remains of animals and plants, as mud, sand, or coarser material. As this sediment is buried deeper by more sediment, it is compacted (pressed down) and cemented by the growth of minerals to form a sedimentary rock. Sandstone, for example, is a sedimentary rock made from cemented sand.

FROM ROCK TO ROCK
As cliffs of sedimentary rocks are eroded, small pieces of rock are deposited on the beach. These will be eroded further and may eventually form new sedimentary rock.

Shell fragment

Thin section of limestone

Finely broken shells

FOSSIL CONTAINER
Many sedimentary rocks contain hard lumps called concretions or nodules. These were formed after the sediment was deposited, often around fossil shells like this clam (p. 26).

Clam shell

FOSSILIFEROUS ROCK
Limestone is a sedimentary rock composed mainly of calcite and a few other similar carbonate minerals. The calcite is usually derived from the broken shells and skeletons of animals and plants that lived in the sea. Larger, more intact shells can also be present, and limestones are therefore good rocks in which to hunt for fossils. This Silurian limestone contains some fossil brachiopods (pp. 24–25).

Fossil brachiopod

Era	Period	Million years ago (mya)
Cenozoic	Holocene (epoch)	0.01
	Pleistocene (epoch)	2
	Pliocene (epoch)	5
	Miocene (epoch)	24
	Oligocene (epoch)	34
	Eocene (epoch)	55
	Paleocene (epoch)	65
Mesozoic	Cretaceous	142
	Jurassic	206
	Triassic	248
Paleozoic	Permian	290
	Carboniferous	354
	Devonian	417
	Silurian	443
	Ordovician	495
	Cambrian	545
	Precambrian (about seven times longer than all the other periods put together)	4,600 (origin of the Earth)

STRATIGRAPHICAL COLUMN
A series of eras and periods (and epochs in the Cenozoic) are used to describe the age of rocks and fossils.

Turning to stone

THE PROCESS OF CHANGING from a living organism to a fossil takes place over millions of years. Fossilization is an extremely chancy process. As soon as animals and plants die, they begin to decompose, or rot. The hard parts – the shells, bones, and teeth of animals; the wood of plants – last longer than soft tissue but are often scattered by animals, wind, or flowing water. In order for something to be fossilized it must be buried quickly before it decomposes, usually by sediment such as sand or mud washed down by water. Some fossils later dissolve; others may be changed chemically or distorted and twisted out of shape by high temperatures and pressures. Only a tiny fraction will survive to be found. The mussel is a good example to show how something can be fossilized.

LAND SHAPES
Over millions of years rocks are eroded and re-shaped, bringing ancient fossils to the surface.

2 DECAYING MUSSEL
When the mussel dies, the two chalky shells open out like butterfly wings. The soft parts of the mussel enclosed by the shells soon begin to rot or are eaten by scavenging animals.

Living mussel

Byssal threads

1 LIVING MUSSEL
Mussels live attached to rocks and other hard surfaces in the sea by byssal threads. The soft parts are enclosed by two chalky shells. Each mussel may spend its entire life in one place, and dense masses form mussel beds. If a mussel becomes detached it may die, especially if it is swept into a different environment.

FROM PRESERVATION TO DISCOVERY
These four drawings show how animals can be preserved and their remains discovered millions of years later. The process is very slow, and the climate and shape of the land probably changes as much as the animal and plant life.

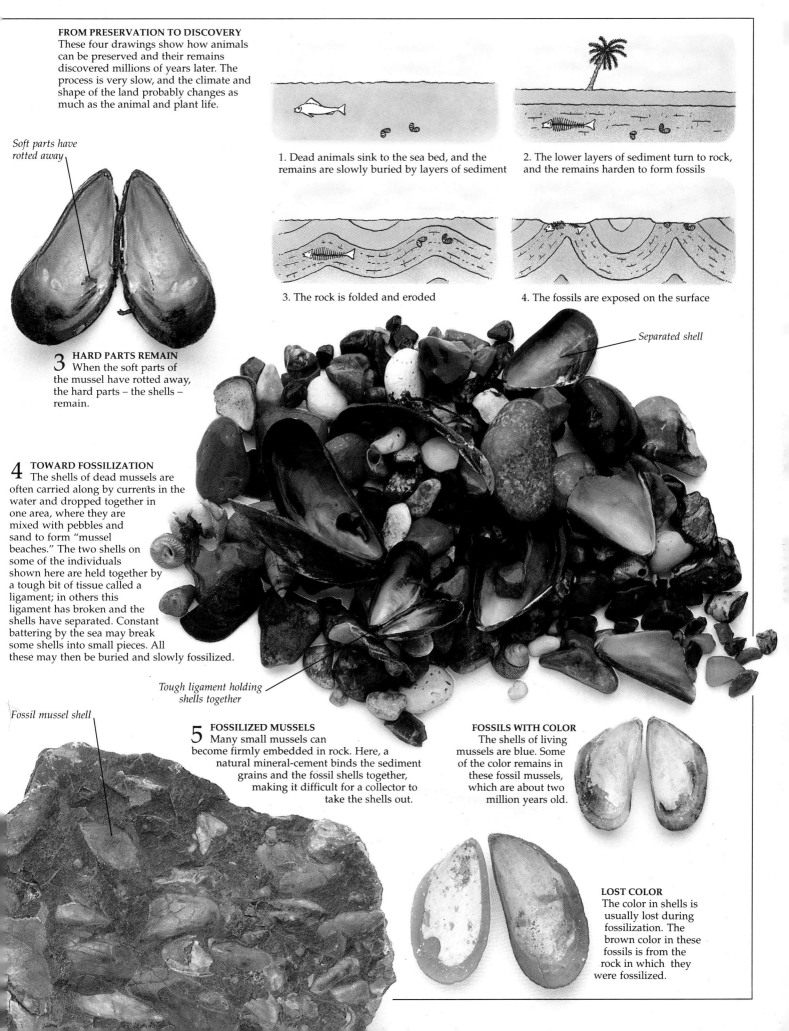

1. Dead animals sink to the sea bed, and the remains are slowly buried by layers of sediment

2. The lower layers of sediment turn to rock, and the remains harden to form fossils

3. The rock is folded and eroded

4. The fossils are exposed on the surface

Soft parts have rotted away

3 HARD PARTS REMAIN
When the soft parts of the mussel have rotted away, the hard parts – the shells – remain.

Separated shell

4 TOWARD FOSSILIZATION
The shells of dead mussels are often carried along by currents in the water and dropped together in one area, where they are mixed with pebbles and sand to form "mussel beaches." The two shells on some of the individuals shown here are held together by a tough bit of tissue called a ligament; in others this ligament has broken and the shells have separated. Constant battering by the sea may break some shells into small pieces. All these may then be buried and slowly fossilized.

Tough ligament holding shells together

Fossil mussel shell

5 FOSSILIZED MUSSELS
Many small mussels can become firmly embedded in rock. Here, a natural mineral-cement binds the sediment grains and the fossil shells together, making it difficult for a collector to take the shells out.

FOSSILS WITH COLOR
The shells of living mussels are blue. Some of the color remains in these fossil mussels, which are about two million years old.

LOST COLOR
The color in shells is usually lost during fossilization. The brown color in these fossils is from the rock in which they were fossilized.

The changing world

THE HISTORY OF LIFE has been played out on a world that has been changing constantly since it was formed about 4,600 million years ago (mya). The Earth's crust is divided into several plates which move relative to one another. Most earthquakes and volcanoes occur along boundaries between these plates. The combined effects of many small plate movements have caused continents to drift across the Earth, to collide and form mountains, and to break into pieces. Continents are still moving today. North America is separating from Europe at a rate of about 0.8 in (2 cm) per year. Sea levels and climates have changed many times. This is why fossils of sea creatures can be found inland, and why fossils of tropical plants can be found where the climate is cold. The maps on these pages show the shape of the land at four stages in geological history. The fossils show a selection of the life that existed during each different time span, and many are featured later in this book.

CONTINUOUS CHANGE
Earthquakes such as the great one of Lisbon, Portugal, in 1755 (above), and the one that devastated Armenia, U.S.S.R., in 1988 show that changes are still taking place on Earth.

Carboniferous mollusk (bellerophontid)

Carboniferous coral

Devonian fish

Carboniferous seed fern

THE OLDEST FOSSILS
The world's oldest fossils are tiny bacteria-like cells 3,500 million years old. Complex animals made of many cells, like this *Tribrachidium* from Australia, appeared at the end of the Precambrian.

Silurian trilobites

Silurian graptolites

Silurian brachiopods

Carboniferous crinoid

Silurian gastropod

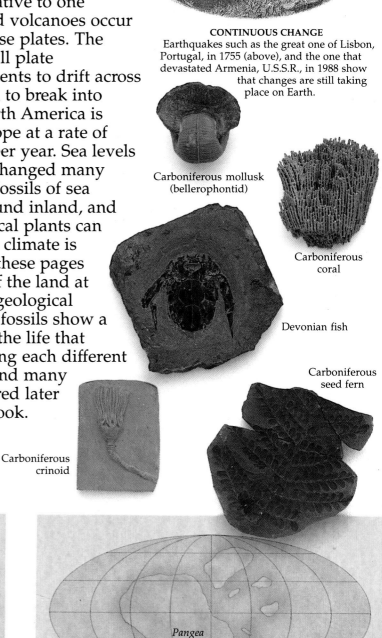

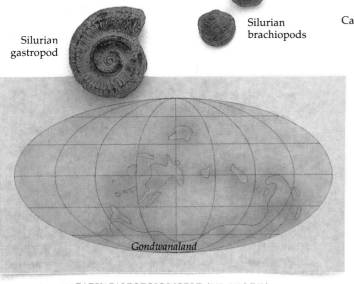

Gondwanaland

Pangea

EARLY PALEOZOIC WORLD (545–418 MYA)
Paleozoic means "ancient life." During the early Paleozoic era (Cambrian, Ordovician, and Silurian periods, p. 9), a large continent, known as Gondwana, was situated over the southern polar region. Most early Paleozoic life was in the sea. Invertebrates (animals without backbones) were especially numerous, but primitive fish were also present. Plants began to live on land toward the end of this time.

LATE PALEOZOIC WORLD (417–249 MYA)
Life diversified greatly during the late Paleozoic era (Devonian, Carboniferous, and Permian periods), at the end of which most of the land was joined in one supercontinent known as Pangaea. Amphibians, reptiles, insects, and other animals colonized the land where they could feed on the vegetation that had evolved. A mass extinction of much of the life occurred at the very end of the Paleozoic.

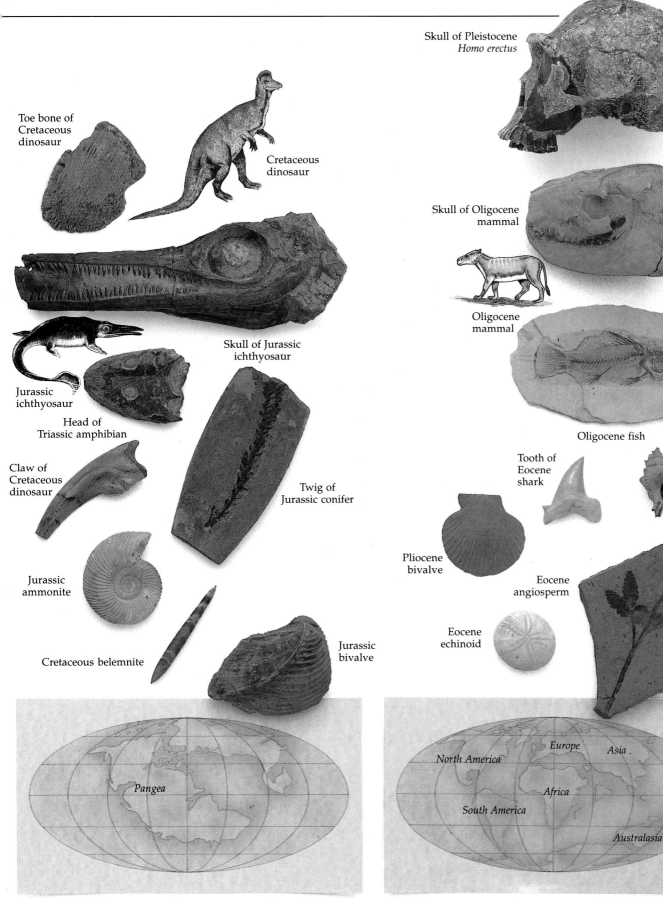

Toe bone of Cretaceous dinosaur

Cretaceous dinosaur

Skull of Pleistocene *Homo erectus*

Skull of Oligocene mammal

Skull of Jurassic ichthyosaur

Oligocene mammal

Jurassic ichthyosaur

Head of Triassic amphibian

Oligocene fish

Claw of Cretaceous dinosaur

Tooth of Eocene shark

Eocene gastropod

Twig of Jurassic conifer

Pliocene bivalve

Eocene angiosperm

Jurassic ammonite

Eocene echinoid

Cretaceous belemnite

Jurassic bivalve

Pangea

North America

Europe

Asia

Africa

South America

Australasia

EARLY PALEOZOIC WORLD (545–418 MYA)
Paleozoic means "ancient life." During the early Paleozoic era (Cambrian, Ordovician, and Silurian periods, p. 9), a large continent, known as Gondwana, was situated over the southern polar region. Most early Paleozoic life was in the sea. Invertebrates (animals without backbones) were especially numerous, but primitive fish were also present. Plants began to live on land toward the end of this time.

LATE PALEOZOIC WORLD (417–249 MYA)
Life diversified greatly during the late Paleozoic era (Devonian, Carboniferous, and Permian periods), at the end of which most of the land was joined in one supercontinent known as Pangaea. Amphibians, reptiles, insects, and other animals colonized the land where they could feed on the vegetation that had evolved. A mass extinction of much of the life occurred at the very end of the Paleozoic.

Early paleontology

THE SERIOUS SCIENTIFIC STUDY OF FOSSILS began only about 300 years ago, although early Greek philosophers such as Pythagoras are reported to have realized the true nature of fossils as long ago as the 5th century B.C. During the Middle Ages in Europe (A.D. 400-1400), many naturalists thought fossils were the products of a mysterious "plastic force" ("*vis plastica*") which formed the fossils within the Earth. Their true origin as the buried remains of ancient animals and plants was established beyond reasonable doubt by Steno (see below) and other naturalists of the 17th century. Fossils were subsequently used to solve geological problems such as the relative ages of different rocks, and also biological problems concerning the evolution and the origin and extinction of various forms of life on Earth. Today scientists throughout the world are still studying fossils, and our understanding of them is increasing all the time.

The frontispiece to the museum catalog of the naturalist Johann Scheuchzer (1672–1733)

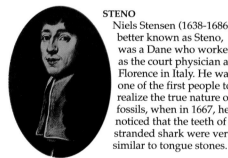

TONGUE STONES
Fossil shark teeth from Cenozoic rocks around the Mediterranean were known to naturalists as tongue stones. Some naturalists believed that they grew naturally within the rocks, but Steno and others realized their correct origins.

STENO
Niels Stensen (1638-1686), better known as Steno, was a Dane who worked as the court physician at Florence in Italy. He was one of the first people to realize the true nature of fossils, when in 1667, he noticed that the teeth of a stranded shark were very similar to tongue stones.

NOAH'S ARK
The Bible story of Noah tells how he took animals onto his ark to escape the great flood. Many naturalists, including Steno, believed that the Biblical Flood had transported and buried fossils. This explained why fossil sea shells occurred on mountaintops. (Scheuchzer once identified the fossil of a salamander as the skeleton of a human drowned in the Flood!)

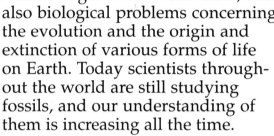

RESTORATION OF *PALAEOTHERIUM*
Cuvier studied *Palaeotherium* bones from the Eocene rocks of Montmartre in Paris. The animal from which they came was restored as this tapir-like mammal.

Grinding teeth of a herbivore

Fossil jaw of *Palaeotherium*

GEORGES CUVIER
The French naturalist Georges Cuvier (1769–1832) made many important contributions to natural history. Early in his scientific career he realized that the different parts of an animal's body were closely interrelated; for example, mammals with horns and hoofs were all herbivores (plant eaters) and would have had the teeth of herbivores. The significance of this observation was that entire animals could now be restored – shown as they would have looked when alive – from the evidence of isolated bones. Cuvier also recognized that many fossils belonged to extinct species, and he devised a view of Earth history in which a succession of catastrophes exterminated earlier forms of life. According to Cuvier, the last of these catastrophes was the Biblical Flood.

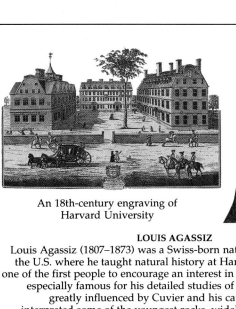

An 18th-century engraving of
Harvard University

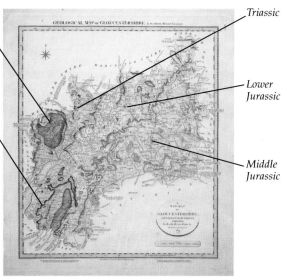

Upper
Carboniferous

Lower
Carboniferous

Triassic

Lower
Jurassic

Middle
Jurassic

LOUIS AGASSIZ

Louis Agassiz (1807–1873) was a Swiss-born naturalist who emigrated to
the U.S. where he taught natural history at Harvard University and was
one of the first people to encourage an interest in paleontology there. He is
especially famous for his detailed studies of fossil fishes. Agassiz was
greatly influenced by Cuvier and his catastrophe theories. He re-
interpreted some of the youngest rocks, widely believed to be deposits
formed by the Biblical Flood, and showed them to have been deposited by
glaciers during the Pleistocene Ice Age.

FIRST USEFUL MAP
William Smith, often regarded as the
father of English geology, produced the
first useful geological maps.

Gastropod

Bivalve
hinge

Gastropod

Gastropod

Bivalve

Ammonite

1. Inoceramus Cuvieri. Thoms. Novak. V. 3p. 448.   4. Ammonites.   7. Terebratula.
2. Inoceramus.   5. Cirrus depressus. Sowerby M.B.   8. Terebratula subundata. M.C. t. 5. f. 7.
3. Cast of the inside of a Trochus.   6. Terebratula.   9. Sharks teeth.

Fig 1 Melania Heddingtonensis Min. Con. t. 39.   Fig 5 Chama   6 Ostrea delta Min. Con. t. 143.
2 Turbo ?   3 Trochus   7 Ammonites

WILLIAM SMITH
The engineer and surveyor
William Smith (1769–1839)
collected fossils from
different rock formations
across England. Some of
the fossils he collected
can be seen here, along
with plates from the
books in which he
illustrated his finds.
Smith saw that
different layers of rock
were characterized by
particular species of
fossils and realized that
rocks containing the same
fossil species must
be of the same
age. Fossils are
still used today
by geologists
to work out the
relative ages of
rocks, helping
them to find
oil and other
valuable
resources.

Fossil folklore

FOLKLORE IS RICH WITH LEGENDS ABOUT FOSSILS. For at least 10,000 years, fossils have figured in the beliefs and customs of people throughout the world. Even today, many people believe that particular types of fossils have supernatural or medicinal powers. Early people apparently valued particular fossils because of their rarity or natural beauty. The origin of fossils was mysterious to people for a long time and led to some peculiar ideas about them. These ideas were passed down from generation to generation and became part of folklore. We now know what the real origin of fossils is, but it is fascinating to see how our ancestors managed to find an explanation for them.

DEVIL'S TOENAIL
The Jurassic oyster *Gryphaea* had a thick curved shell which is still popularly known as a Devil's toenail. This name was given to it in spite of the fact that the Devil has usually been described as having hoofs rather than toes!

An artist's idea of the Devil

Carved snake's head

Snakestone (ammonite)

Whitby coat of arms

Ancient Whitby coin

SNAKESTONES
Ammonites (pp. 28–29) from Whitby in England were believed to be the remains of coiled snakes turned to stone by the 7th-century abbess St. Hilda. Craftsmen carved heads onto some ammonites to help with this belief. Three snakestones are included in the Whitby coat of arms, seen on this ancient coin.

Thunderstones (fossil sea urchins)

MAGIC STONES
There are many legends about fossil sea urchins (pp. 32–33). Some people thought they were thunderstones which fell from the sky during a thunderstorm. They were believed to keep milk from going sour. One type was thought to be hardened balls of froth made by entwined snakes at midsummer. The snakes tossed them in the air, and if someone caught one in a cloth it had great magical powers (right).

Woodcut of 1497

TOADSTONES
The shiny, button-shaped fossil teeth of the Mesozoic fish *Lepidotes* (p. 35) were believed to come from within the heads of toads. This woodcut illustration from 1497 shows the supposed removal of one.

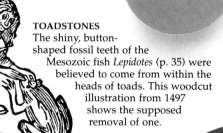

TOADSTONE MEDICINE
In Europe during the 1400s, toadstones were thought to cure epilepsy and counter poison.

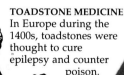

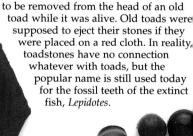

OLD TOAD'S TALE
To be used as medicine, toadstones had to be removed from the head of an old toad while it was alive. Old toads were supposed to eject their stones if they were placed on a red cloth. In reality, toadstones have no connection whatever with toads, but the popular name is still used today for the fossil teeth of the extinct fish, *Lepidotes*.

Toadstones (fossil fish teeth)

FAMOUS MYTH
This illustration showing the mythical unicorn is a detail from a French tapestry called *The Lady and the Unicorn*, dating from about 1500.

Unicornum verum (fossil mammoth tusk)

REAL UNICORN
The tusk of a small whale called the narwhal was for many years identified as the horn of the unicorn. However, the discovery in about 1600 of some fossil mammoth tusks led to *these* being proclaimed as the true horns of unicorns, or *unicornum verum*.

LUCKY SPINES
These are the club-shaped spines of the sea urchin *Balanocidaris*. They can be found in Cretaceous rocks in an area in the Middle East that used to be called Judea hence their name of Jewstones. They were used as good luck charms as long ago as 650 B.C.

Natural hole through sponge

Porosphaera

SPONGE BEADS
Bronze Age people in Britain made necklaces by stringing together certain fossil sponges. Some specimens of the Cretaceous sponge *Porosphaera* are remarkably like beads. Many even have a natural hole through the middle, probably caused by the sponge's having grown around part of another creature or plant.

BRONZE AGE BURIAL
The skeletons of this woman and her child were found buried on Dunstable Down, England. Around the grave were three rows of fossil sea urchins, buried with the woman and child about three thousand years ago, maybe to ward off evil spirits.

Thunderbolts (belemnites)

Stone swallow (fossil brachiopod)

THUNDERBOLTS
These are the internal shells of extinct squidlike animals called belemnites (p. 29). In folklore they were thought to have been flung down as darts from the heavens during thunderstorms, and they supposedly had medicinal powers. Belemnites have also been found with human skeletons in ancient burial mounds.

TAKE ONE SHELL
In China the fossil shells of certain brachiopods (p. 25) are called *Shiyyen* (stone swallows) and are still used as medicine. According to the prescription supplied with these Devonian brachiopods, they should be ground up, baked in a clay pot, and taken as a cure for many illnesses including rheumatism, cataracts, anemia, and digestive problems. The medicine is described as sweet and cooling.

京都 永仁
堂 仁 石燕
總蹏北平王府井大街電東五零號
支店烟台北大街電話四百六十四
甘焉
主赤白帶下
去湿止淋
治腸風痔瘻
眼目障膜

Fossils of the future

THE FOSSIL RECORD is a highly selective sample of ancient life. Many creatures rotted away entirely because they did not have resistant hard parts. Some lived in environments where burial and fossilization were unlikely to occur; for example, in treetops. Others lived in oceans, lakes, and rivers where fossilization was more likely. Yet, even in these environments, only a small proportion of life would have been fossilized. This selectivity is well illustrated by looking at a modern community to see which animals and plants might become fossils of the future.

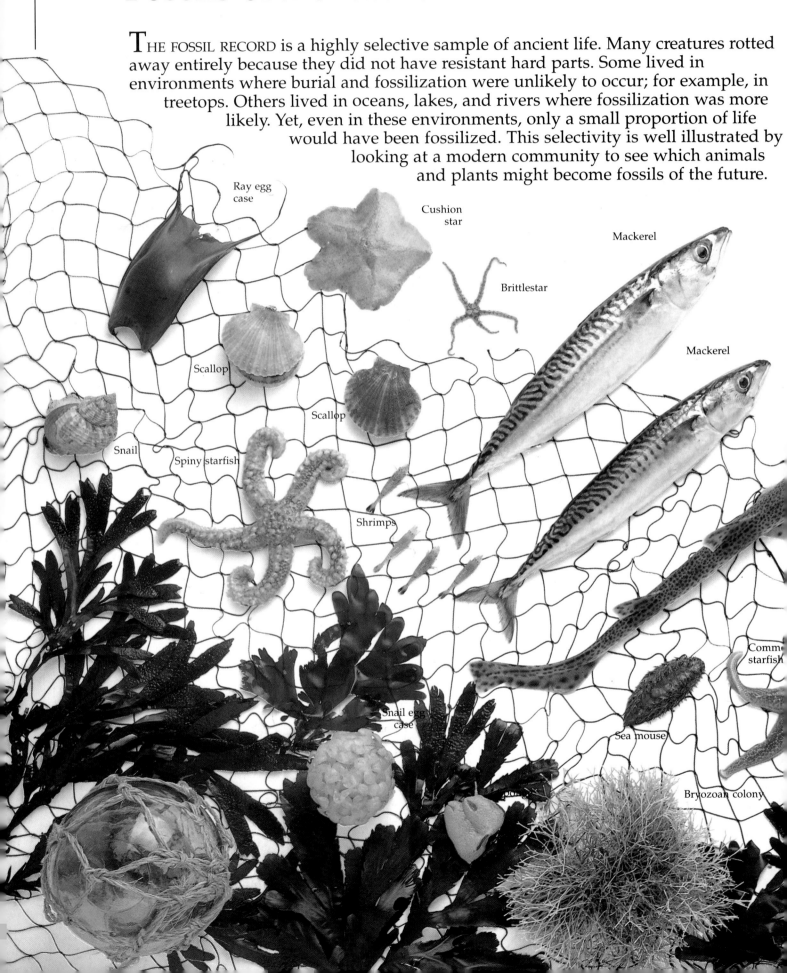

Ray egg case

Cushion star

Brittlestar

Mackerel

Mackerel

Scallop

Scallop

Snail

Spiny starfish

Shrimps

Snail egg case

Sea mouse

Comm starfish

Bryozoan colony

Mackerel skeletons

TEMPORARY TENANT
A good example of a creature that is unlikely to leave direct evidence of its existence is the hermit crab. Hermit crabs are unusual in having no shell of their own. They use abandoned snail shells as homes. In some habitats every available snail shell contains a hermit crab. Much of a hermit crab's body is soft and it twists in the spiral of the snail shell. The claws are hard but are rarely fossilized and are almost never found within the shell occupied by the crab. This is probably because decay of the organic material in the claws causes them to disintegrate before fossilization. However, when looking at fossil snail shells, it is worth bearing in mind that they may have had two tenants – a snail and a hermit crab.

Dogfish teeth   **Crab shell**

Scallop shells

Snail shell

Edible sea urchin skeleton   **Green sea urchin skeleton**

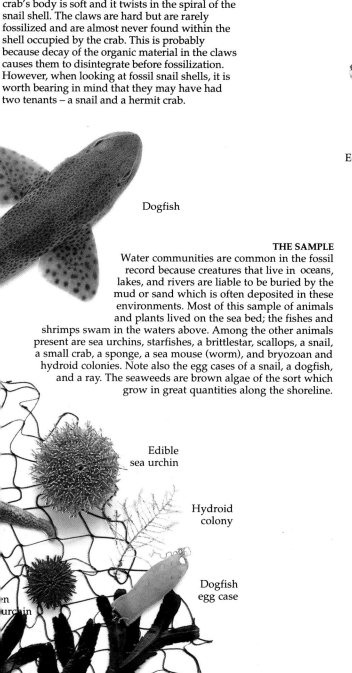

Dogfish

THE SAMPLE
Water communities are common in the fossil record because creatures that live in oceans, lakes, and rivers are liable to be buried by the mud or sand which is often deposited in these environments. Most of this sample of animals and plants lived on the sea bed; the fishes and shrimps swam in the waters above. Among the other animals present are sea urchins, starfishes, a brittlestar, scallops, a snail, a small crab, a sponge, a sea mouse (worm), and bryozoan and hydroid colonies. Note also the egg cases of a snail, a dogfish, and a ray. The seaweeds are brown algae of the sort which grow in great quantities along the shoreline.

Common starfish skeleton   **Cushion star skeleton**   **Spiny starfish skeleton**

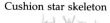

Brittlestar skeleton

THE REMAINS
The parts of animals that are most likely to be fossilized are the hard parts such as teeth, bones, and shells. The hard parts of the sample of animals and plants are shown together here. The seaweeds and many of the animals have disappeared entirely. Others have left very little trace. All that remains of the dogfish, for example, are its teeth. A dogfish has a skeleton of nonresistant cartilage, not bone. The sea urchins, starfishes, brittlestar, crab, and bryozoans had resistant skeletons. However, these consisted of many separate pieces which have now mostly fallen apart as the soft tissues connecting them decayed. Only the snail and scallop shells have survived with little obvious change. The mackerel bones and crab shell would probably decay before fossilization unless buried very rapidly because they contain a lot of organic material. This illustrates dramatically how little of a modern community would usually survive to be fossilized. The same was true for communities of the geological past.

Bryozoan skeletons

Edible sea urchin

Hydroid colony

Dogfish egg case

n urchin

Crab

LEAVING NO TRACE
Animals and plants living and dying on land often decay completely before they can be buried and fossilized. The fur and flesh of this reindeer carcass, photographed in the Arctic, are beginning to rot away from the bones. These too will disintegrate unless by chance they are buried.

Remarkable remains

FOSSILS OF SOFT TISSUES, which usually decay during fossilization, are sometimes found. These include entirely soft-bodied animals which are otherwise unrepresented in the fossil record. Fossilization of soft parts is of great importance because it supplies much more information about the living animals than do bones, teeth, or shells. Discoveries of preserved humans are always exciting and include those at Pompeii in Italy and Grauballe in Denmark.

Skin traces

Part   IN TWO PARTS   Counterpart

The outline of the body is clearly shown in this fossilized frog. Even traces of the skin and other fleshy tissues have been preserved. The rock has split straight through the preserved animal, leaving the fossil in two pieces known as the part and counterpart.

STICKY DEATH
A spider can clearly be seen in this piece of amber, the fossilized resin of an ancient plant. Amber often contains animals that were trapped in the sticky resin as it dripped down trunks and stems. Insects, spiders, and even small lizards and frogs have been preserved for millions of years in this way.

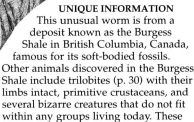

UNIQUE INFORMATION
This unusual worm is from a deposit known as the Burgess Shale in British Columbia, Canada, famous for its soft-bodied fossils. Other animals discovered in the Burgess Shale include trilobites (p. 30) with their limbs intact, primitive crustaceans, and several bizarre creatures that do not fit within any groups living today. These animals were buried in mudflows on the Cambrian sea bed over 500 million years ago, and their fossils provide us with a unique glimpse of a very varied early community.

EXCEPTIONAL INSECT
This delicate dragonfly was buried in mud which formed the Solnhofen Limestone of Bavaria, West Germany, a deposit renowned for its exceptional fossils.

DEEP-FROZEN MAMMOTH
Mammoths have occasionally been recovered from the permafrost (permanently frozen ground) of Siberia, northern Asia. They were probably trapped and frozen when they fell into cracks in glaciers. Mammoths lived during the Ice Ages of the last two million years and became extinct about 12,000 years ago. The largest species grew to over 13 ft (4 m) at the shoulder.

ACTIVE VOLCANO
The famous volcano Vesuvius in southeast Italy has erupted frequently over the years. It has been quiet since 1944 but is not thought to be extinct.

Cast of body from Pompeii

BURIED IN ASH
During the violent eruption of Mount Vesuvius in A.D. 79, inhabitants of the nearby towns of Pompeii and Herculaneum were buried beneath avalanches of volcanic ash and debris. The bodies lasted long enough for the ash to harden around them, and when they decayed they left cavities. The cavities were excavated and then filled with plaster to make casts, which gruesomely revealed victims' postures at the moment of death. Some bodies of pets have also been found.

SOFT PRESERVATION *left*
Belemnoteuthis from the Jurassic is related to squid, cuttlefish, and the extinct belemnites (p. 29). The internal skeleton of this specimen is hidden beneath the soft body, which has been preserved because of replacement by the mineral apatite soon after death and burial. Even the hooked tentacles around the head can be seen. Ink was released from a sac as a defensive screen, an ability that *Belemnoteuthis's* relatives possess today.

Hooked tentacles

Bone

Skin

Fossil moa foot

Preserved soft body hides the internal skeleton

The cast of the body shows exactly how this person was lying when buried by ash over 1,900 years ago

Claw

SKINNY CLAW
The moas of New Zealand were large flightless birds related to the kiwi, emu, and ostrich. The biggest was 11 ft (3.5 m) tall. Although now extinct, moas were alive when Maoris first lived in New Zealand 700 years ago. Fossils of many different species of moa have been found, some over two million years old. This fossilized foot still has skin attached. The impact these once dominant birds had on New Zealand's native vegetation is still evident today in plants that have evolved a resistance to being eaten by moas!

A moa among kiwis

Reconstruction of a mammoth stuck in the tar at La Brea

STUCK FAST
Tar oozing naturally to the surface at La Brea in Los Angeles, California, has entombed many animals accidentally caught in the sticky substance over the past 10,000 to 20,000 years. Excavations in the older solidified layers of tar have unearthed the bones of extinct mammals such as mammoths and saber-toothed cats (p. 55).

GRAUBALLE MAN
Human bodies in remarkable states of preservation have been excavated from several peat bogs in northern Europe. The acid material of the bogs prevented the total decay of soft parts. Many bodies are over 2,000 years old, and some show signs of a ritual killing. This man was found in 1952 near the village of Grauballe in Denmark. He died in about the 4th century. Skin and internal organs – even remains of his last meal – have been preserved.

Corals

CORALS ARE SOME OF THE MOST BEAUTIFUL ANIMALS in the sea. The colorful massed tentacles of coral individuals, or polyps, resemble flowers in an undersea garden. Most corals live in warm, shallow, tropical waters and feed on plankton but also obtain nutrition from algae which may live within their bodies. Corals may be solitary (living by themselves) or colonial (many polyps joined together). Fossil corals are common because beneath the soft-bodied polyps are hard, chalky skeletons. The oldest are from the Ordovician. Related sea anemones and jellyfish lack hard skeletons and are seldom fossilized.

CORAL FISHING
Coral has long been collected for its beauty and is used in jewelry.

A ring-shaped coral reef is called an atoll

Separate corallite

Individual coral skeleton

Red limestone

PIPE CORAL
This is a colony of *Acrocyathus*, a Carboniferous coral. The pipe-shaped corallites (skeletons formed by individual polyps) grew separately. The spaces between them are now filled with red limestone.

HORN CORAL
Aulophyllum, shown here in two pieces, is a typical solitary coral. It lived on the sea bed, growing in this characteristic horn shape. The pointed end was buried in sediment on the sea bed, and the soft polyp sat on top of the other end.

PACKED COLONY
Lonsdaleia is a colonial coral which belongs to a group called the Rugosa. Rugose corals became extinct in the Permian. The individual corallites which make up the colony are many-sided, usually hexagonal (six-sided), because they are so tightly packed together.

MODERN CORALS
Most modern corals belong to a group called the scleractinians which first appeared in the Triassic. Coral reefs are inhabited by countless numbers of different animals and are the most diverse marine environments.

Pale sediment filling areas once occupied by soft tissues

Branch of corallites

CHAIN CORAL
The corallites of the Silurian coral *Halysites* are arranged in long branching ribbons. On the surface, the coral looks like a collection of chains.

BRAIN CORAL
Together, the individuals of brain corals form winding valleys, and the colonies resemble human brains. Polyps may share a common mouth with others in the same valley. This Miocene example has been cut horizontally and polished to show the inside.

Winding valley of coral

RECORD-BREAKING CORAL
This fossilized fragment is of the reef-building coral *Galaxea*. The structure of the individual skeletons can easily be seen. The world's largest known living coral is a *Galaxea* colony from Okinawa in Japan. It has a circumference (outer boundary) of 52 ft (16 m).

CORAL BUSH
Colonies of the coral *Thamnopora* are bush-shaped, with corallites opening all over the surfaces of the branches. This example is in a piece of limestone which has been cut across horizontally and polished to show the shape of the colony.

Individual coral skeleton

Fossil Fungia

SOLITARY CORALS
These unusual-looking fossils are the delicate skeletons of the solitary corals *Stephanophyllia* and *Fungia*, which lived on the sea bed in the Pliocene and Pleistocene respectively. As their name suggests, the skeletons of *Fungia* look like the undersides of mushrooms.

REPLACED CORAL
The skeletons of some fossil corals are made of the mineral aragonite. Aragonite dissolves easily, so the skeletons often disappear during fossilization. In this fossil colony of *Thecosmilia* the skeletons have been replaced by silica.

Skeleton replaced by silica

Fossil Stephanophyllia

Sea bed dwellers

CLOSE NEIGHBORS
Bryozoan colonies can be compared to blocks of apartments and other buildings containing several similar homes.

Aᴍᴏɴɢ ᴛʜᴇ ᴍᴏsᴛ ᴄᴏᴍᴍᴏɴ ғᴏssɪʟs to be found are the remains of animals and plants which lived on the sea bed. They lived where sand and mud were regularly deposited, and most of the animals had hard parts which could survive decay and be fossilized. The plants and many of the animals could not escape burial, even when they were alive, because they lacked the ability to move. Bryozoans and brachiopods are living examples of this type of animal but because they live in the sea, many people are not aware of their existence. Today, there are only 250 known species of brachiopods. This contrasts with the huge numbers – about 30,000 – of known fossil species.

Holes in the colony through which water and food particles are pumped

ARCHIMEDES' SCREW
This distinctive Carboniferous bryozoan is named after a spiral water pump invented by the Greek mathematician Archimedes. The screw-shaped skeleton once supported a twisted net of individuals similar to *Hornera* (center left).

Archimedes' water pump

Each piece is a colony containing at least 200 individuals

COMMUNITY HOMES *above*
Because of their branching shape, this type of modern bryozoan, *Hornera*, often provides a home for worms, small fishes, and many other animals in the sea.

One individual skeleton

Free-living colonies of Cretaceous bryozoans

Light and dark growth bands

LARGER THAN LIFE
The calcite skeletons of individuals in a bryozoan colony are magnified here many times.

Calcite colonies

Bryozoans are tiny animals which live in colonies where each individual is attached to its neighbor. A colony may contain tens, hundreds, or even thousands of individuals, each one less than 0.04 in (1 mm) long. They have tentacles which they use to feed on tiny particles of food. Most have calcite skeletons. Colonies, which grow by budding new individuals, vary in shape. Some are flat sheets; others grow upright and look like nets or bushes.

BEETROOT STONE
The red color of the Jurassic alga *Solenopora* is sometimes preserved, and these fossils are then known as beetroot stones.

OLD LACE
The fragments of lace bryozoan (*Chasmatopora*) in this Ordovician shale are among the oldest known bryozoans.

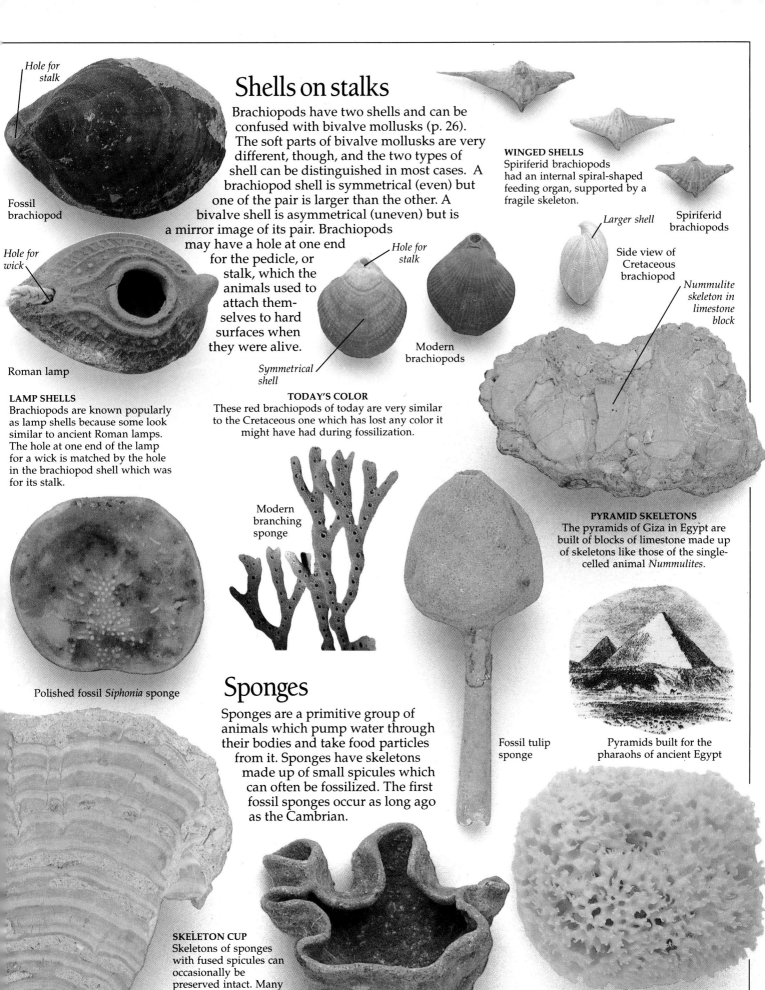

Hole for stalk

Fossil brachiopod

Hole for wick

Roman lamp

Shells on stalks

Brachiopods have two shells and can be confused with bivalve mollusks (p. 26). The soft parts of bivalve mollusks are very different, though, and the two types of shell can be distinguished in most cases. A brachiopod shell is symmetrical (even) but one of the pair is larger than the other. A bivalve shell is asymmetrical (uneven) but is a mirror image of its pair. Brachiopods may have a hole at one end for the pedicle, or stalk, which the animals used to attach themselves to hard surfaces when they were alive.

Hole for stalk

Modern brachiopods

Symmetrical shell

TODAY'S COLOR
These red brachiopods of today are very similar to the Cretaceous one which has lost any color it might have had during fossilization.

WINGED SHELLS
Spiriferid brachiopods had an internal spiral-shaped feeding organ, supported by a fragile skeleton.

Larger shell

Spiriferid brachiopods

Side view of Cretaceous brachiopod

Nummulite skeleton in limestone block

LAMP SHELLS
Brachiopods are known popularly as lamp shells because some look similar to ancient Roman lamps. The hole at one end of the lamp for a wick is matched by the hole in the brachiopod shell which was for its stalk.

Modern branching sponge

Polished fossil *Siphonia* sponge

Sponges

Sponges are a primitive group of animals which pump water through their bodies and take food particles from it. Sponges have skeletons made up of small spicules which can often be fossilized. The first fossil sponges occur as long ago as the Cambrian.

Fossil tulip sponge

PYRAMID SKELETONS
The pyramids of Giza in Egypt are built of blocks of limestone made up of skeletons like those of the single-celled animal *Nummulites*.

Pyramids built for the pharaohs of ancient Egypt

SKELETON CUP
Skeletons of sponges with fused spicules can occasionally be preserved intact. Many are cup-shaped like this Cretaceous example.

Sponge skeleton treated to make a bath sponge

Shells of all shapes

AT THE BEGINNING of the Cambrian Period, about 545 million years ago, complex animals with hard shells and skeletons first appeared in the sea. Among these were the mollusks, a group of animals that are still abundant today. Gastropods, or snails, and bivalves such as clams, mussels, and oysters are the most familiar mollusks, but other kinds include chitons and cephalopods (p. 29). Bivalves have two shells, or valves, joined together by a hinge, while gastropods only have one shell. The shells of mollusks are often found as fossils. Most are made of calcite, or of aragonite, which dissolves more easily. Internal molds of mollusks are often found where aragonite shells became filled with sediment before the shells themselves dissolved.

VENUS'S SHELL
The Roman goddess Venus emerging from a scallop shell.

Pearl

ANCIENT JEWELS
This mudstone contains rare fossil pearls. They are from the Eocene, and are about 50 million years old.

Hinge tooth

Muscle scar

HINGED TOGETHER
Hinge teeth help hold a bivalve's shells together when it is alive. This shell belonged to an Eocene bivalve, *Venericardia*.

GOOD EYESIGHT
Scallops have many eyes, each of which has well-developed focusing lenses. The eyes are situated in soft tissue near the edge of the shells, which are hinged together. To feed, scallops open their shells and use their gills to force a current of water, laden with food particles, through the "gape" in the shells.

Shell *Eye* *Gape*

Sensory tentacles

SPINES FOR SPONGES
The "thorny oyster" *Spondylus* is so named because of its spiny shell, as seen in this Pliocene specimen. Spines of modern *Spondylus* help sponges and other encrusting animals grow on their shells, which protects the bivalve from predators.

Prominent rib

FALLING APART
These fossilized shells, one flat, the other convex (domed), belong to the scallop *Pecten* from the Pliocene. The prominent ribs on the two shells interlock, but, as with many bivalve fossils, the shells are usually found separated because the connecting ligament rots away.

CARVED IN STONE
An ancient Arabic prayer has been carved on these two fossils. They are internal casts (p. 6) of bivalves, formed by sediment which solidified in the space between the shells.

Modern Cone
shell

Fossil Cone
shell

Modern snail shell

Fossil snail shells

DISAPPEARING COLOR
Some living gastropods, especially those of the tropics, are often brightly colored because of chemical substances within the shell called pigments. Unfortunately, pigments are usually destroyed during fossilization.

Siphon

Foot

SOFT-HEARTED
This modern sea-snail is just emerging from its shell. Parts of its soft body can clearly be seen (at top and bottom right).

Modern snail

Curious coils

Gastropod shells of all ages come in many different shapes and sizes. They are all open at one end and are usually twisted into a spiral coil with a gradually increasing diameter. The exact shape of the spiral varies according to the species. It can be left-handed, right-handed, loosely coiled or tightly coiled, regular or irregular. The coiling of the shell on the freshwater snail *Planorbis* is almost flat. The shell of *Turritella* is drawn out into a high spire.

Spiral coil

Fossil
Turritella

"WORM SHELLS"
Vermetids are unusual for gastropods as they attach themselves permanently to a hard surface, often in clusters like these fossil examples. Their shells are irregularly coiled and look more like worms.

Fossil chiton

Modern
chiton

NO CONNECTION
Chitons are a small group of marine mollusks with shells made up of eight individual plates. Fossil chitons are rare and their plates are disconnected. Today, chitons can be found in tide pools, clinging to the sides of the rocks from which they scrape algae for food.

Left-handed coil

Right-handed coil

LOOSE COILS
Tubina is a very unusual type of mollusk which belonged to a now-extinct group called the bellerophontids. It has a loosely coiled shell and dates from the Devonian Period. It is uncertain whether *Tubina* was a true gastropod or not because its soft body has not been preserved.

SPIRAL FOSSILS
Most gastropod shells have a right-handed spiral coil, such as *Neptunea despecta*. The shell of *Neptunea contraria* has a left-handed coil.

Fossil *Neptunea
contraria*

Fossil *Neptunea
despecta*

Siphonal canal

EXTRA LONG
The pointed shell of *Fusinus* is further lengthened by a siphonal canal which the animal used in respiration.

Top

Fossil *Planorbis*

Underneath

Intelligent mollusks

An ammonite with its shell partly replaced by iron pyrites

DECORATIVE MOTIF
The beautiful shape of ammonites is often used in decoration. This is a column from a terraced house in Brighton, England. The architect's name was Amon!

THE OCTOPUS, SQUID, and cuttlefish are modern representatives of a group of sea-dwelling mollusks called cephalopods, which have left a rich fossil record. Cephalopods are regarded as the most highly developed mollusks. They have suckered tentacles, eyes that are remarkably similar to more advanced vertebrate animals, and the ability to learn and use their learning. They are active predators, moving quickly through the water using a type of jet propulsion. Most modern cephalopods have internal shells completely covered by soft parts. However, like the living *Nautilus*, many fossil cephalopods, including the ammonites, had external shells that were similar to the shells of snails but were divided into chambers. Following their first appearance in the Cambrian, many different species of cephalopods came and went, making them very useful fossils for dating rocks (p. 9).

IMPORTANT EVIDENCE
As the only living nautiloid, *Nautilus* is the closest modern relative of the ammonites, and provides us with important clues about this extinct group. *Nautilus* is a nocturnal animal, active only at night, and lives in the Pacific Ocean at depths ranging from 16 to 1,800 ft (5 to 550 m). Its prey consists of fish and crustaceans which it eats with its hard beak.

Septa dividing shell into chambers

Final chamber

Complex suture line

Ammonites

VARIOUS SIZES
Some Mesozoic ammonites reached gigantic sizes. This large specimen, about 12 in (30 cm) wide, is small compared to giants which could be 6 ft (2 m) in diameter.

Simple suture line

Fossil nautiloids

ROOMS FOR EXPANSION
Fossil ammonites and nautiloids have coiled shells divided into a series of chambers by membranes called septa. Only the final chamber next to the opening was occupied by the animal. As it grew, the animal periodically moved forward and formed new septa at the rear of the body chamber. Older chambers were filled with liquid and gas, the proportions of which could be changed through a canal called the siphuncle to allow the animal to move up and down in the sea. Suture lines, formed where the septa meet the shell, are simple in nautiloids but are folded into complex saddles and lobes in ammonites.

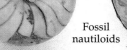

Male ammonite

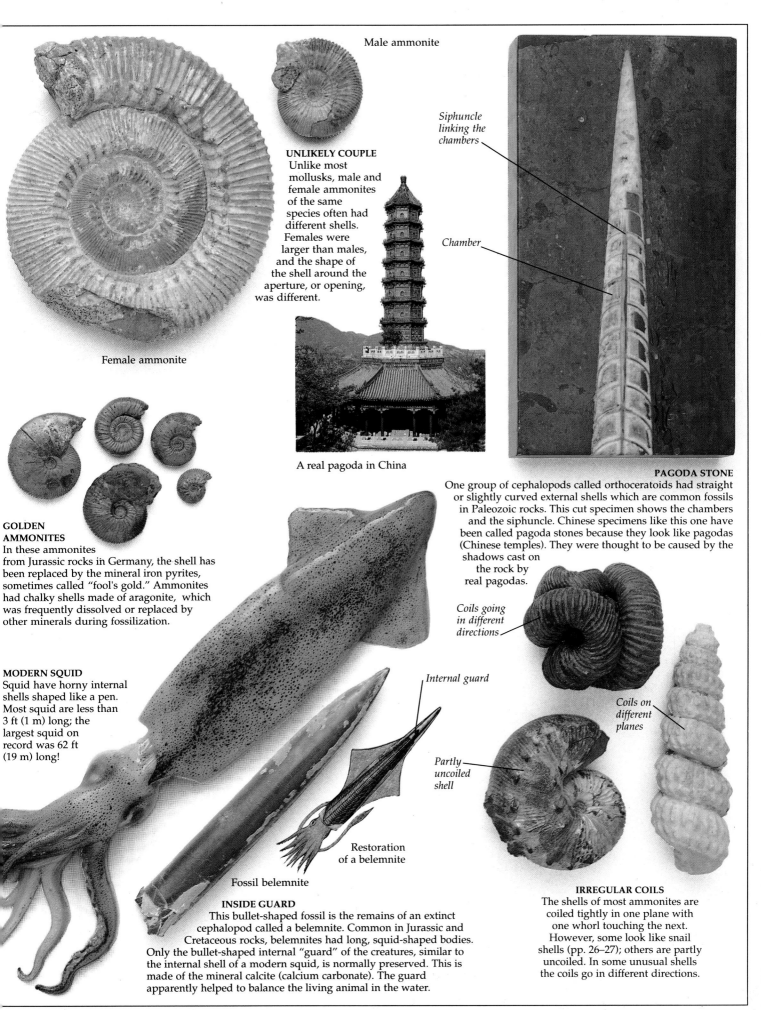

UNLIKELY COUPLE
Unlike most mollusks, male and female ammonites of the same species often had different shells. Females were larger than males, and the shape of the shell around the aperture, or opening, was different.

Female ammonite

A real pagoda in China

Siphuncle linking the chambers

Chamber

PAGODA STONE
One group of cephalopods called orthoceratoids had straight or slightly curved external shells which are common fossils in Paleozoic rocks. This cut specimen shows the chambers and the siphuncle. Chinese specimens like this one have been called pagoda stones because they look like pagodas (Chinese temples). They were thought to be caused by the shadows cast on the rock by real pagodas.

GOLDEN AMMONITES
In these ammonites from Jurassic rocks in Germany, the shell has been replaced by the mineral iron pyrites, sometimes called "fool's gold." Ammonites had chalky shells made of aragonite, which was frequently dissolved or replaced by other minerals during fossilization.

MODERN SQUID
Squid have horny internal shells shaped like a pen. Most squid are less than 3 ft (1 m) long; the largest squid on record was 62 ft (19 m) long!

Coils going in different directions

Coils on different planes

Internal guard

Partly uncoiled shell

Restoration of a belemnite

Fossil belemnite

INSIDE GUARD
This bullet-shaped fossil is the remains of an extinct cephalopod called a belemnite. Common in Jurassic and Cretaceous rocks, belemnites had long, squid-shaped bodies. Only the bullet-shaped internal "guard" of the creatures, similar to the internal shell of a modern squid, is normally preserved. This is made of the mineral calcite (calcium carbonate). The guard apparently helped to balance the living animal in the water.

IRREGULAR COILS
The shells of most ammonites are coiled tightly in one plane with one whorl touching the next. However, some look like snail shells (pp. 26–27); others are partly uncoiled. In some unusual shells the coils go in different directions.

Animals in armor

Insects, spiders, crabs, scorpions, lobsters, millipedes, barnacles, and many other animals belong to a major group of animals called arthropods, a word which means "jointed foot." Some arthropods live in the sea, some live on land, and some fly; but very few are found as fossils. All arthropods have jointed legs, a segmented body, and an exoskeleton, or outer armor. As the animal grows, it has to shed its exoskeleton every so often and grow another one. Some arthropods – the extinct trilobites, for example – have the mineral calcite in their exoskeletons, making them resistant to decay. These exoskeletons are the parts of arthropods most commonly found fossilized.

PRIZE POSSESSION
Trilobites are prized fossils. This Silurian *Calymene* has been made into a brooch. Examples of this species were found in such great numbers at Dudley, England, that they were nicknamed Dudley bugs.

SMALL IS BEAUTIFUL
Most trilobites were 1 to 4 in (3 to 10 cm) long. These are examples of *Elrathia*.

Eyes

No eyes

TO SEE OR NOT TO SEE?
There were more than 10,000 different species of trilobites and all of them lived in the sea. Some crawled along the sea bed, others floated or swam through the water. Most species had two eyes and could probably see very well. Lenses are sometimes preserved in fossil trilobites because they were made of the mineral calcite. Some species, however, were eyeless. Most of these lived in darkness in the deep sea, beyond the depth to which natural light penetrates.

Trilobite *Dalmanites*

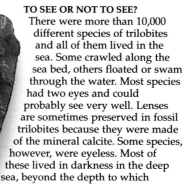

Trilobite *Concoryphe*

Modern millipede

Fossil millipede

EARLY SETTLERS
Like all arthropods, millipedes have bodies divided into segments, or sections. Unlike the other arthropods on these pages, they live on land and were among the first animals to do so. Fossil millipedes are seldom found.

Packed lenses

MULTIVISION
Trilobite eyes are the most ancient visual systems known. They consisted of many separate lenses packed together. Each lens produced its own image.

Echinocaris, a Devonian shrimplike arthropod

ROLL UP!
Some trilobites were able to roll up like wood lice, probably for protection against predators.

TRI-LOBED
The name "trilobite" was given to these creatures because their exoskeletons are divided into three distinct parts or lobes. The legs on the lower surface of the animal and the soft parts were very rarely preserved. Whole fossil trilobites are surprisingly rare, but they can be found in rocks from the Cambrian to the Permian Period, about 545 to 248 million years old. They became extinct after that. This one is *Paradoxides* from the Cambrian. One of the biggest of all trilobites, it grew to 1 ft 7 in (50 cm) long.

Long spine

PRICKLY CUSTOMER
This Devonian trilobite, *Dicranurus*, was notable for its long spines, which are superbly preserved in this specimen.

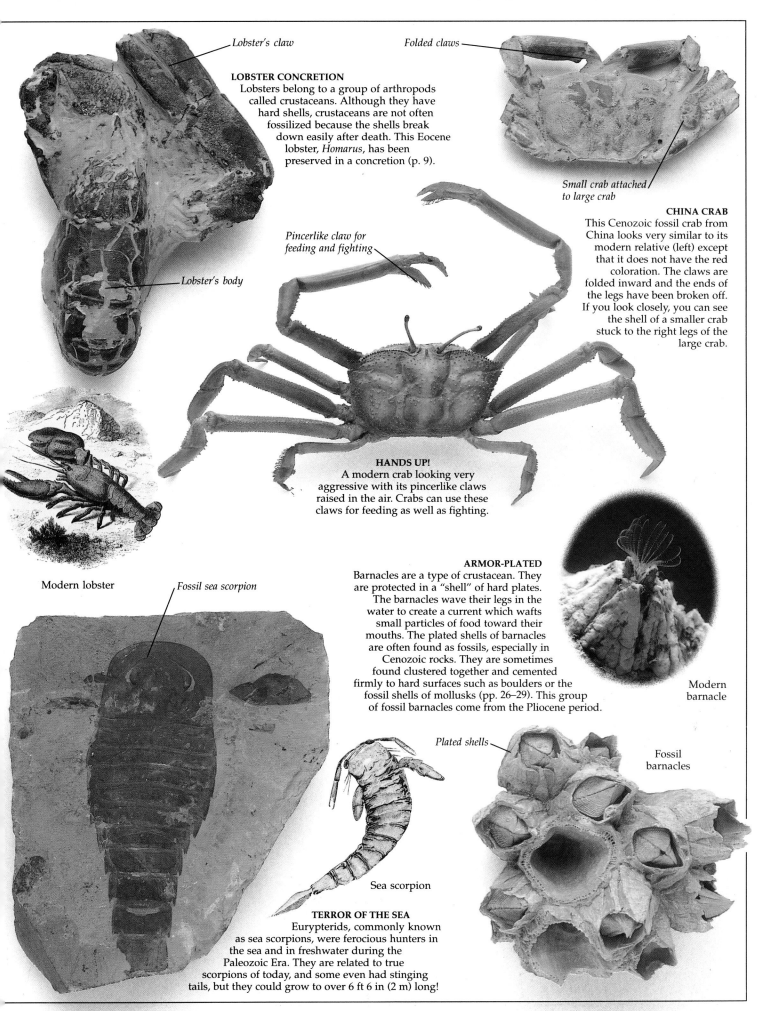

Lobster's claw

LOBSTER CONCRETION
Lobsters belong to a group of arthropods called crustaceans. Although they have hard shells, crustaceans are not often fossilized because the shells break down easily after death. This Eocene lobster, *Homarus*, has been preserved in a concretion (p. 9).

Lobster's body

Folded claws

Small crab attached to large crab

CHINA CRAB
This Cenozoic fossil crab from China looks very similar to its modern relative (left) except that it does not have the red coloration. The claws are folded inward and the ends of the legs have been broken off. If you look closely, you can see the shell of a smaller crab stuck to the right legs of the large crab.

Pincerlike claw for feeding and fighting

HANDS UP!
A modern crab looking very aggressive with its pincerlike claws raised in the air. Crabs can use these claws for feeding as well as fighting.

Modern lobster

Fossil sea scorpion

ARMOR-PLATED
Barnacles are a type of crustacean. They are protected in a "shell" of hard plates. The barnacles wave their legs in the water to create a current which wafts small particles of food toward their mouths. The plated shells of barnacles are often found as fossils, especially in Cenozoic rocks. They are sometimes found clustered together and cemented firmly to hard surfaces such as boulders or the fossil shells of mollusks (pp. 26–29). This group of fossil barnacles come from the Pliocene period.

Modern barnacle

Plated shells

Fossil barnacles

Sea scorpion

TERROR OF THE SEA
Eurypterids, commonly known as sea scorpions, were ferocious hunters in the sea and in freshwater during the Paleozoic Era. They are related to true scorpions of today, and some even had stinging tails, but they could grow to over 6 ft 6 in (2 m) long!

Arms and spines

ECHINODERMS are a very distinctive group of animals which all live in the sea. Among them are sea urchins (echinoids), sea lilies (crinoids), starfish (asteroids), and brittlestars (ophiuroids). The distinguishing feature of most echinoderms is their fivefold radial symmetry. That is, their bodies can be divided into five similar segments, kind of like the segments of an orange. As echinoderms have skeletons made of calcite, they are often found fossilized. Indeed, fossil echinoderms range back to the Cambrian. Echinoderm skeletons consist of many individual pieces or plates, each grown as a single crystal of calcite. These are often separated and scattered soon after the animal dies, so rapid burial is especially important to ensure good preservation.

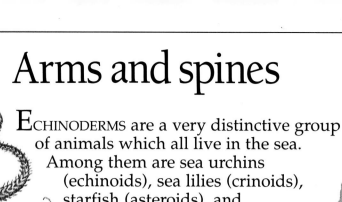

Modern brittlestar

Delicate interlinked arms

BURIED ALIVE
This exceptional Jurassic specimen shows a group of five fossil brittlestars with arms interlinked. These may have been buried while still alive, as the plated skeletons are normally scattered soon after death. Brittlestars look like starfish but are more delicate and their arms break off easily, hence their name. They use their arms to move across the sea bed. Some feed on plankton; others are scavengers.

Symmetrical arm

STAR HUNTER
Many starfish are very efficient hunters, often feeding on clams and oysters which they open using the suckers on their arms. Others, like this Australian *Protoreaster*, extract their food from sediments such as sand.

Modern *Protoreaster*

STAR OF THE BEACH
Starfish are familiar to anyone who has explored tide pools and beaches by the sea, but they are very seldom found as fossils.

Position of missing arm

Mouth

Ammonite

Mouth

Suckers

Underside of modern starfish

ARM ROBBERY
This fossil starfish from the Jurassic, seen from underneath, is remarkably similar to some present-day species but unfortunately one of its arms is missing. Its mouth can be seen in the center. The rock in which it is embedded contains small ammonites and many shell fragments as well.

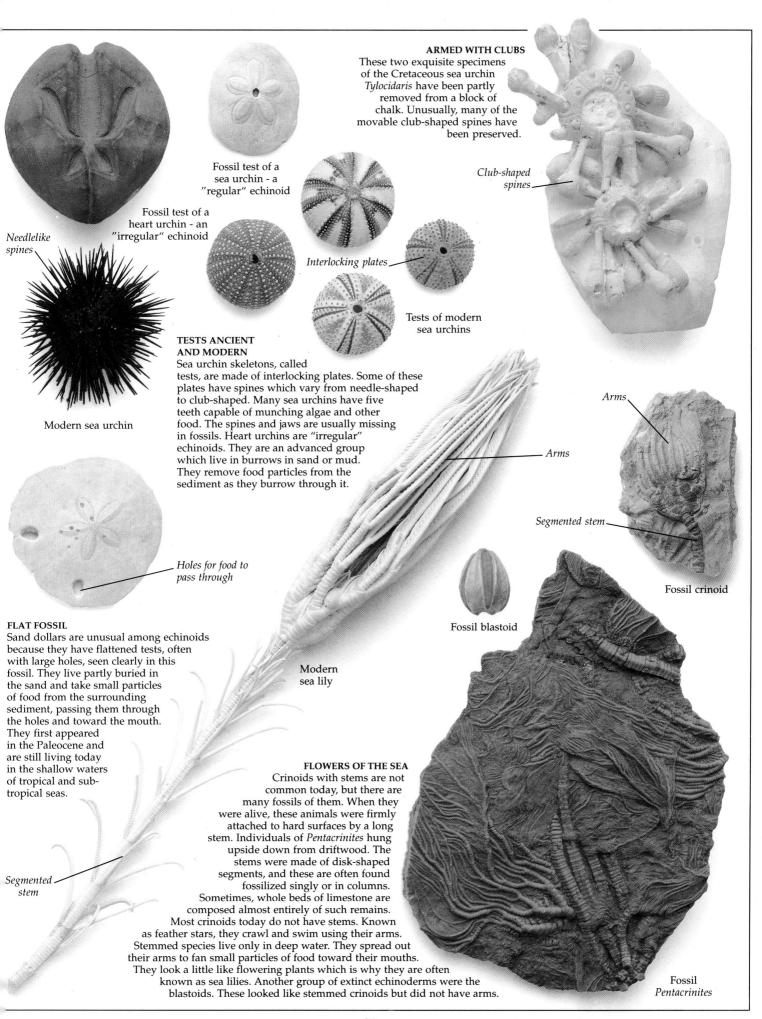

ARMED WITH CLUBS
These two exquisite specimens of the Cretaceous sea urchin *Tylocidaris* have been partly removed from a block of chalk. Unusually, many of the movable club-shaped spines have been preserved.

Club-shaped spines

Fossil test of a sea urchin - a "regular" echinoid

Fossil test of a heart urchin - an "irregular" echinoid

Needlelike spines

Interlocking plates

Tests of modern sea urchins

Modern sea urchin

TESTS ANCIENT AND MODERN
Sea urchin skeletons, called tests, are made of interlocking plates. Some of these plates have spines which vary from needle-shaped to club-shaped. Many sea urchins have five teeth capable of munching algae and other food. The spines and jaws are usually missing in fossils. Heart urchins are "irregular" echinoids. They are an advanced group which live in burrows in sand or mud. They remove food particles from the sediment as they burrow through it.

Arms

Arms

Fossil crinoid

Segmented stem

Fossil blastoid

Holes for food to pass through

FLAT FOSSIL
Sand dollars are unusual among echinoids because they have flattened tests, often with large holes, seen clearly in this fossil. They live partly buried in the sand and take small particles of food from the surrounding sediment, passing them through the holes and toward the mouth. They first appeared in the Paleocene and are still living today in the shallow waters of tropical and sub-tropical seas.

Modern sea lily

FLOWERS OF THE SEA
Crinoids with stems are not common today, but there are many fossils of them. When they were alive, these animals were firmly attached to hard surfaces by a long stem. Individuals of *Pentacrinites* hung upside down from driftwood. The stems were made of disk-shaped segments, and these are often found fossilized singly or in columns. Sometimes, whole beds of limestone are composed almost entirely of such remains. Most crinoids today do not have stems. Known as feather stars, they crawl and swim using their arms. Stemmed species live only in deep water. They spread out their arms to fan small particles of food toward their mouths. They look a little like flowering plants which is why they are often known as sea lilies. Another group of extinct echinoderms were the blastoids. These looked like stemmed crinoids but did not have arms.

Segmented stem

Fossil *Pentacrinites*

Fishes

FISHES are the most primitive vertebrates (animals with backbones). They are a very varied group, with about 20,000 species, and they use gills to breathe and fins to swim. Some fishes live in the sea and some in fresh water; others migrate between these environments. Fishes first appeared about 500 million years ago. Most were small, jawless, and covered with heavy armor. In the Devonian period, often referred to as the Age of Fishes, fishes became numerous, and early representatives of the major living groups were present. Skeletons of fossil fishes can be abundant in certain areas, but it is more common to find isolated teeth, especially of sharks.

Sparnodus part

FIN SPINE
Sharks and rays have skeletons made of cartilage, which is softer than bone and not usually fossilized. However, fossils of their teeth and spines stretch back to the Devonian. This is the spine of a Jurassic shark. It supported a large fin on the shark's back.

Dorsal fin

Impression of a modern shark

Sharp teeth

Teeth of an Eocene sand shark, *Eugomphodus*

ARMORED FISHES
One of the first known fishes with jaws was a group of armored fishes called placoderms. Some used their two arms to prop themselves up on the beds of rivers and freshwater lakes.

TOOTH FOR A TOOTH
Most sharks are fierce predators with a mass of sharp teeth arranged in whorls. New teeth are growing all the time to replace older teeth that drop out. The largest modern shark on record, a great white, was 29 ft 6 in (9 m) long. This is small in comparison with its extinct relative, *Carcharodon*, whose tooth (right) is 4 in (11 cm) long, suggesting a body length of over 39 ft (12 m).

Tooth of Pliocene shark, *Carcharodon*

Modern ray

Ptychodus tooth

Ridges for crushing food

Ridged Ptychodus tooth

JAWLESS FISHES
Cephalaspids were primitive freshwater fishes. They were jawless, and fed by sucking sediment from lakes or riverbeds.

SHELL CRUSHERS
Fossil teeth like these are all that is known of the cartilaginous fish *Ptychodus*, which was probably similar to a modern ray. It had ridged teeth, which it used to crush the shells of the mollusks on which it fed.

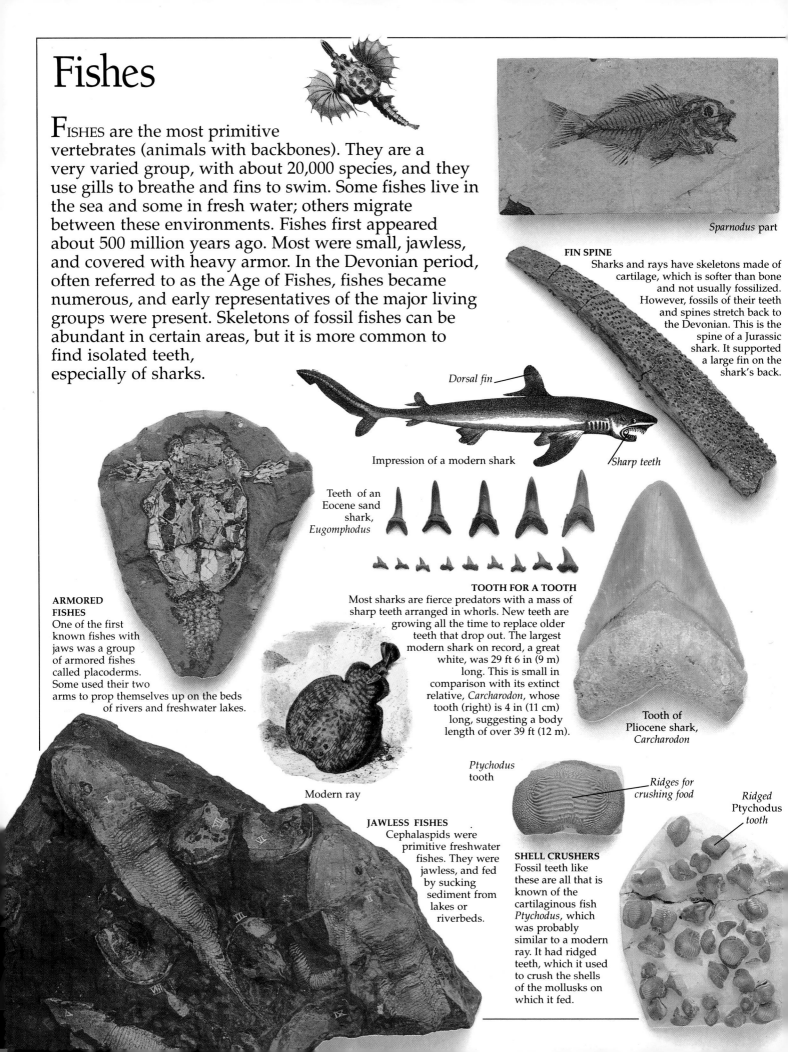

Well-preserved skeleton

FISH EATS FISH *right*
Fossils seldom provide direct evidence of an animal's diet. However, this remarkable Cretaceous dogfish contains the head of a teleost that it swallowed. The dogfish had very small teeth and would probably not have been able to bite the head off the body of a live fish. It seems more likely that the dogfish scavenged the head from a dead fish.

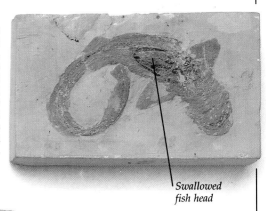
Swallowed fish head

Sparnodus counterpart

TWO PARTS
This slab of Eocene limestone has split through a fine fossil specimen of *Sparnodus*. The two pieces are called the part (left) and the counterpart (above). Bones of the skeleton, including the fins, are preserved in remarkable detail. *Sparnodus* belongs to a group of bony fishes still living today, known as porgies or sea breams.

THICK-SCALED FISH
Lepidotes was a Mesozoic bony fish. It was common all over the world, and some examples grew to a length of almost 6 ft 6 in (2 m). The body was covered by thick scales, and the button-shaped teeth, called toadstones in folklore (p. 16), were probably used to crush mollusk shells.

Thick scales covering the body

Sharp predator's teeth

EAR STONES
Otoliths, or ear stones, are balance organs from the ears of fishes. They are made of chalky material and form unusual fossils. These examples are from Eocene fishes.

Modern African lungfish

TEETH FOR HUNTING
Related to the modern bowfin, *Caturus* is from the Jurassic. By the look of its sharp teeth it was a predator.

Armored head

Thick scales

BONY FISHES
About 200 million years ago, this primitive teleost, a type of bony fish, lived in the seas. It had small teeth, which suggests that it fed on tiny plankton, possibly living in schools like today's herring. Teleosts first appeared in the Triassic, and today they are the most common fishes. They include carp, salmon, cod, mackerel, flounder, and many others.

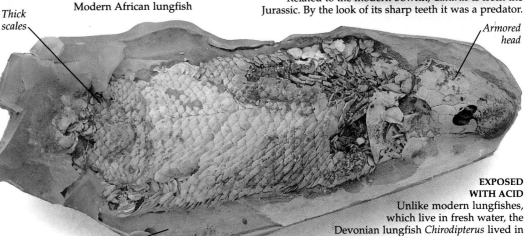
Remains of concretion

EXPOSED WITH ACID
Unlike modern lungfishes, which live in fresh water, the Devonian lungfish *Chirodipterus* lived in shallow seas. It had thick, bony scales and an armored head. This specimen from Australia was preserved in a hard, chalky concretion (p. 9). It has been exposed by treatment in acid, which dissolved the concretion but not the fish within.

Plants-the pioneers

THE INVASION OF THE LAND BY PLANTS about 440 million years ago was a key event in the history of life. It paved the way for colonization by animals and was the starting point for the development of the variety of plants we see today. Plants growing on the land had to be strong enough to support themselves against gravity, resistant to drying, and able to transport water, gathered by the roots, up to the higher portions of the plant, where energy-producing photosynthesis occurred. These adaptations were first seen among the primitive land plants such as club mosses, horsetails, and ferns of the late Paleozoic. Examples from all of these groups are living today, though often in greatly reduced numbers. The flowering plants that dominate modern floras did not appear until the Cretaceous.

JET JEWELRY
Jet is a special kind of fossil wood which is dense enough to be carved and polished for jewelry. The formation of jet probably occurred when wood from monkey puzzle trees (opposite) was washed into the sea by rivers.

Impression in sandstone of the bark of *Lepidodendron*

JOHANN SCHEUCHZER
The Swiss naturalist and physician Johann Scheuchzer (1672–1733) studied fossil plants and fishes from the Miocene rocks at Oeningen in Switzerland.

Diamond-shaped leaf scars

Lepidodendron

Cross-section of the fossil cone *Lepidostrobus*

Fossil *Baragwanathia*

Club mosses

Club mosses, which belong to a group of plants called lycopods, reproduce by spores which are held in cones. Lycopods were common during the Paleozoic; *Baragwanathia* from the Devonian of Australia is probably the oldest known example. Some modern club mosses have creeping stems, unlike the Paleozoic lycopods which grew as trees. *Lepidodendron* reached 130 ft (40 m) tall. The fossil bark of *Lepidodendron* has a diamond pattern on it made by scars left when the leaves fell off. The fossil cones of *Lepidodendron* have been named *Lepidostrobus*.

Carboniferous club moss *Archaeosigillaria*

Modern club moss *Lycopodium*

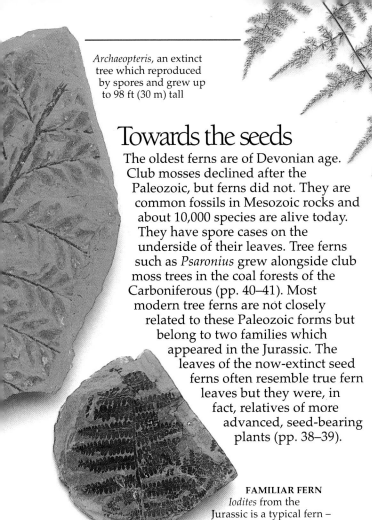

Archaeopteris, an extinct tree which reproduced by spores and grew up to 98 ft (30 m) tall

Modern plant showing fern-like features

Towards the seeds

The oldest ferns are of Devonian age. Club mosses declined after the Paleozoic, but ferns did not. They are common fossils in Mesozoic rocks and about 10,000 species are alive today. They have spore cases on the underside of their leaves. Tree ferns such as *Psaronius* grew alongside club moss trees in the coal forests of the Carboniferous (pp. 40–41). Most modern tree ferns are not closely related to these Paleozoic forms but belong to two families which appeared in the Jurassic. The leaves of the now-extinct seed ferns often resemble true fern leaves but they were, in fact, relatives of more advanced, seed-bearing plants (pp. 38–39).

COMPRESSED FERN
Carbonized (turned to coal) leaves of the Jurassic fern *Coniopteris* are here preserved as compressions.

FAMILIAR FERN
Iodites from the Jurassic is a typical fern – the fronds are very similar to many modern species.

Plants in a typical Paleozoic scene

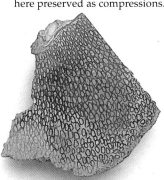

POLISHED FERN
This sectioned and polished piece of fossil wood is from the tree fern *Psaronius*, which grew to a height of 26 ft (8 m).

FOSSIL MONKEY PUZZLE CONES
One cone has been sectioned to show the internal structure.

WIDESPREAD SEED FERN
The presence of fossils of this seed fern, *Glossopteris*, in India, Africa, South America, Australia, and Antarctica provides evidence that these areas were once linked together as Gondwanaland (pp. 12–13).

The only modern horsetail genus, *Equisetum*, which grows to about 5 ft (1.5 m) tall

Leathery leaf

Leaf-bearing part of stem

MONKEY PUZZLE
The monkey puzzle is a primitive type of conifer (pp. 38–39) first appearing in the Triassic. Today they live in the Andes mountains in South America. The tightly packed leathery leaves may live for 15 years before falling off the branch.

HORSETAILS
Horsetails date from the Devonian. Some grew as trees in the coal forests (pp. 40–41), reaching heights of 60 ft (18 m). This is the stem of a Jurassic *Equisetites*.

Equisetites

Modern monkey puzzle branch

Underground part of stem

Continued on next page

Protected seeds

Most modern seed-producing plants have their seeds protected in a fruit (flowering plants, called angiosperms) or a cone (gymnosperms, including conifers). Angiosperms are the most successful of modern plants. There are an estimated 250,000 species, as compared with 50,000 species of all other plants. Grasses, oaks, tulips, palms, potatoes, and cacti are angiosperms. In spite of their great variety, angiosperms appear relatively late in the fossil record. The earliest examples come from the Cretaceous. The earliest conifer fossils occur earlier, in the Carboniferous.

SOFT FRUIT
All fruits contain seeds of some sort. Soft fruits decay quickly. Hard seeds are more likely to be fossilized.

Palm-like leaf

Fossil cycad

BEFORE THE FLOWERS
When angiosperms first appeared, some of the most common plants were cycads – palmlike gymnosperms which produced seeds in separate conelike structures. Modern cycads still look like palms. There are nine kinds living in tropical and subtropical forests.

Annual rings preserved in stone

Petrified conifer wood

CYCAD COMPANION
Other gymnosperms were also living at this time, and some Cretaceous conifer wood has been petrified (turned to stone). Petrification has preserved remarkable details of the original wood.

Sabal leaf

FOSSIL PALM
There are two main types of angiosperms - monocotyledons and dicotyledons. Monocotyledons generally have leaves with parallel veins; dicotyledons usually have net-veined leaves. Palms, like this *Sabal* from the Eocene, are monocotyledons, as are grasses. All other angiosperms shown are dicotyledons.

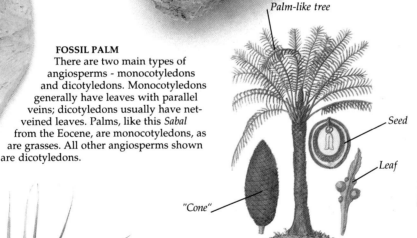

Palm-like tree

Seed

Leaf

"Cone"

Modern cycad

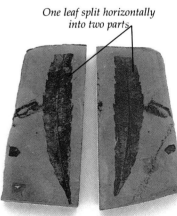

One leaf split horizontally into two parts

SPLIT IN TWO
Angiosperm leaves are relatively common and well preserved in some fine-grained sedimentary rocks. This Miocene example of a myrtle leaf has been fractured into two parts.

Leaf of a modern palm

Fossil *Nipa* fruit

COAST GUARDS
A fruit of a modern *Nipa* tree is compared here with a smaller fossil *Nipa* fruit from the Eocene. *Nipa* is a stemless palm which grows today along tropical coastlines or rivers close to the coast. It plays an important role in preventing coastal erosion.

Modern *Nipa* fruit

FLAT CHESTNUT
This is the flattened seed of a water chestnut from the Miocene.

continued from previous page

Fossil poplar leaf

SMALL CHANGE
Fossil poplar leaves are almost identical to present-day poplar leaves. This beautiful example is about 25 million years old. Modern poplar trees can grow to 130 ft (40 m) tall; during its lifetime, each tree sheds a huge number of leaves that could become fossils.

Modern poplar leaves

Juglans seeds

Palliopora seeds

Mastixia seeds

Tectocarya seeds

Greatly magnified fossil pollen

FIRST POLLEN
This Cretaceous pollen grain is one of the earliest-known types of angiosperm pollen.

ANCIENT SEEDS
Angiosperm seeds are often enclosed in a fleshy fruit eaten by animals, which then scatter the seeds. Various types of fossil fruits and seeds are common from the late Cretaceous onward. All those shown here are about 30 million years old.

GIANT CONIFER
Giant redwoods are conifers now only living in North America. Remains can be found in Jurassic and younger rocks. Conifers are gymnosperms; that is, they produce seeds inside cones. Fossils include rooted stumps and fallen trunks as well as cones and seeds.

Fossil Miocene leaves

Fossil maple leaf showing midrib and veins

LEAVES IMPRESSIONS
These Miocene leaves are beautifully preserved as impressions in a fine-grained limestone. The three-lobed leaf with midrib and delicate veins is easy to identify as that of a maple, even though very little of the original plant tissue remains.

Leaves of a modern maple

Bud

BUDDING MAPLE
Buds are rarely preserved in fossil plants but, remarkably, one is attached to this flattened twig of a Miocene maple tree.

STONE RINGS
Growth rings, like those that can be seen in the wood of trees living today, show clearly in this polished section of petrified oak wood. They provide useful information about the seasonal growth of the tree, and the climate at the time the tree was living.

Fossil flower

PRESERVED PETALS
Although fossils of flowering plants are common, the flowers themselves are seldom found, since they are delicate and short-lived. Therefore, these petals of *Porana* from the Miocene are exceptional. A flower of today with similar petals is the primrose.

Growth rings

Modern primrose

Fossil fuels

Living mosses and grasses

Oıl ᴀɴᴅ ᴄᴏᴀʟ are known as fossil fuels because they originate from ancient organisms, mainly plants. When we burn them we release the energy, in the form of heat and light, which was originally captured by the living plants during photosynthesis millions of years ago. Fossil fuels are extracted from the Earth in huge quantities. In addition to being a source of energy, they are also used in the manufacture of many synthetic materials.

A coal forest

COAL PLANT
This is the impression of the bark of one of the plants which lived in the vast coal forests of the Carboniferous. About two-thirds of the world's coal supplies were formed by the plants of these forests.

PEAT
The plants growing on top of this peat will eventually die and add their rotting remains to the peat beneath. Dried peat is sometimes used as a household fuel.

Crack caused when drying

LIGNITE
Lignite, the first stage of coal formation, is typically dark brown and may still contain some water. Lignite crumbles easily and may crack as it dries in the air.

From plant to coal

Coal is formed after millions of years by the decay and burial of plants that usually grow in freshwater swamps. Special conditions are needed for coal to form. During the early stages of the process, oxygen must not be present so that bacterial decay of the plants can lead to the formation of peat. The peat is then buried and compressed under the weight of more sediment and rotting plants. It undergoes chemical changes resulting first in lignite, then bituminous coal, and finally, if temperatures and pressures become sufficiently high, anthracite coal.

MODERN MINING
Most coal is extracted by deep mining. When the coal is near the surface, it is extracted by strip mining.

Impression of lycopod bark

COAL LABOR
Wagons full of coal were once hauled through the underground tunnels by men, women, and children. Nowadays, there are conveyor belts, or trucks pulled by engines.

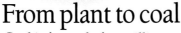

Ink

Shoe polish

BITUMINOUS COAL
Black bituminous coal is sometimes used as a fuel for household heating. The impression of a Carboniferous lycopod tree (p. 36) seen here shows the plant origin of the coal.

ALL MADE FROM COAL
Most coal is burned to provide heat or to make steam which, in turn, is used to drive the generators in power stations producing electricity. But many everyday products used in the home and garden are also made from coal. These include coal-tar soap, ink, and shoe polish. Other products sometimes made from coal are antiseptics, drugs, dyes, detergents, perfumes, nail polish, fertilizers, weed-killers, insecticides, nylon, and plastics.

Coal-tar soap

ANTHRACITE
Anthracite is a hard, intensely black and shiny coal. It is the best-quality coal.

OIL PLANT

This is a greatly enlarged fossil of a microscopic Eocene plant which lived in the sea. Similar planktonic plants were the originators of oil. Their fossilized remains provide important clues about rocks, useful to geologists searching for oil.

NO OIL

This core of rock, cut during drilling for geologists to examine, does not contain any oil.

OIL-BEARING

This dark piece of porous core does contain oil. Oil does not form huge underground lakes but is held as tiny droplets in the pores in the rock – as water is held in a sponge.

Light crude oil

REFINED OIL

Oils are treated in a refinery. Refining is a very complex process involving several different stages.

From plankton to oil

Oil and natural gas are together known as petroleum, from the Latin words *petra* (rock) and *oleum* (oil). They were formed mainly by the decomposition of tiny planktonic plants which lived near the surface of the sea. When they died, their remains sank to the sea bed and were buried in mud. Over millions of years, this mud turned to rock, and the organic remains formed specks of carbon-rich kerogen, an early stage of oil, and then oil. Oil is often found some distance away from where it originated. It migrates, or moves, generally upward through porous rocks which have tiny spaces into which it can seep. If it meets an impervious layer of rock – that is, rock which has no pores – the oil cannot migrate. It may therefore become trapped in what is then called a "reservoir rock."

Modern oil rig

Heavy crude oil

CRUDE OILS

It can be extremely difficult to get oil out of rock. Often, the presence of natural gas helps force the oil up to the surface, but sometimes pressure is too low and the oil has to be pumped up. Crude oils – oils in their natural state – vary widely. The heaviest oils, formed at relatively low temperatures, are black, thick, and waxy. The lightest oils, formed at high temperatures, are pale and thin. All crude oils must be refined before they can be used.

Crayons

ALL MADE FROM OIL

Once in the refinery, oil is separated into different liquids, gases, and solids. These are used to make a wide range of products in addition to gasoline, diesel fuel, and lubricating oil. Many detergents, paints, plastics, and clothes are derived from petroleum chemicals. These crayons, sunglasses, and polyester scarf are all byproducts of oil.

Three cones of the bit

DRILLING FOR OIL

The most common drill bit is a tri-cone bit like this one. Bits cut through rock by being rotated at the bottom of a hollow drill pipe down which a muddy fluid is pumped. This fluid lubricates and cools the bit and carries away the fragments of rock.

An early way of drilling for oil

Polyester scarf

Sunglasses

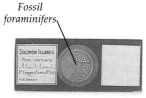

Fossil foraminifers

MICROSCOPIC FOSSILS

Fossils of foraminifers – microscopic animals with chalky shells – are often used by geologists to date rocks.

Out of the water

Fleshy outline of the body

COLONIZATION OF THE LAND by vertebrates 350 million years ago was made possible through the evolution of lungs for breathing air, and limbs for walking. Air-breathing was inherited by the first land vertebrates, amphibians, from their fish ancestors. Fishes with lungs for breathing – lungfishes (p. 35) – still exist today. The Australian lungfish can gulp fresh air from the surface of drying ponds while other fishes die in the foul water. Limbs for walking developed from muscular fins similar to those seen in the living coelacanth (p. 61). Most amphibians have a larval stage (tadpole) which has to live in water, and for this reason amphibians must return to water to lay their eggs.

Long hind legs

CURIOUS CREATURE
This curious amphibian, *Diplocaulus*, from the Permian of Texas, lived in ponds and streams.

Eyes

FOSSIL FROG
This fossil frog is a female of a species of *Discoglossus*. It comes from the Miocene of West Germany. The specimen is unusual in showing the fleshy outline of the body and long hind legs. Frogs first appeared in the Triassic but are seldom found fossilized because their delicate bones decay very easily.

FOSSIL TADPOLE
Even rarer than fossils of adult frogs are fossils of their tadpoles. The two eyes can be clearly seen in this Cenozoic specimen of *Pelobates*.

ETERNAL YOUTH
The axolotl is an unusual salamander from Central America. It remains in a "larval" stage throughout its life, using its feathery external gills to breathe underwater and not coming onto land. The name axolotl comes from an appropriate Aztec word meaning "water doll."

GOING THROUGH STAGES
Like most amphibians, frogs usually have to lay their eggs in water. These hatch into tadpoles that live in the water. As they develop, tadpoles go through different stages before they leave the water as miniature frogs. Lungs and skin replace gills as a means of breathing, fore- and hind legs grow, and the tail gradually disappears.

Heavy hip bones

SURVIVING AMPHIBIAN
The early inhabitants of the land differed in many ways from the amphibians which have survived to the present day such as frogs, toads, newts, and salamanders. This is a modern natterjack toad.

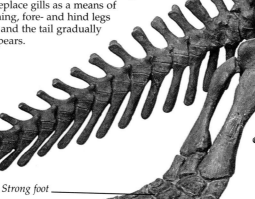

Strong foot

EARLY ANCESTOR
One of the earliest known amphibians, *Ichthyostega*, is found in Devonian rocks in Greenland. It is regarded by some paleontologists as an ancestor of all later amphibians. It was apparently able to walk on land and had lungs for breathing air, but still had a tail fin like a fish.

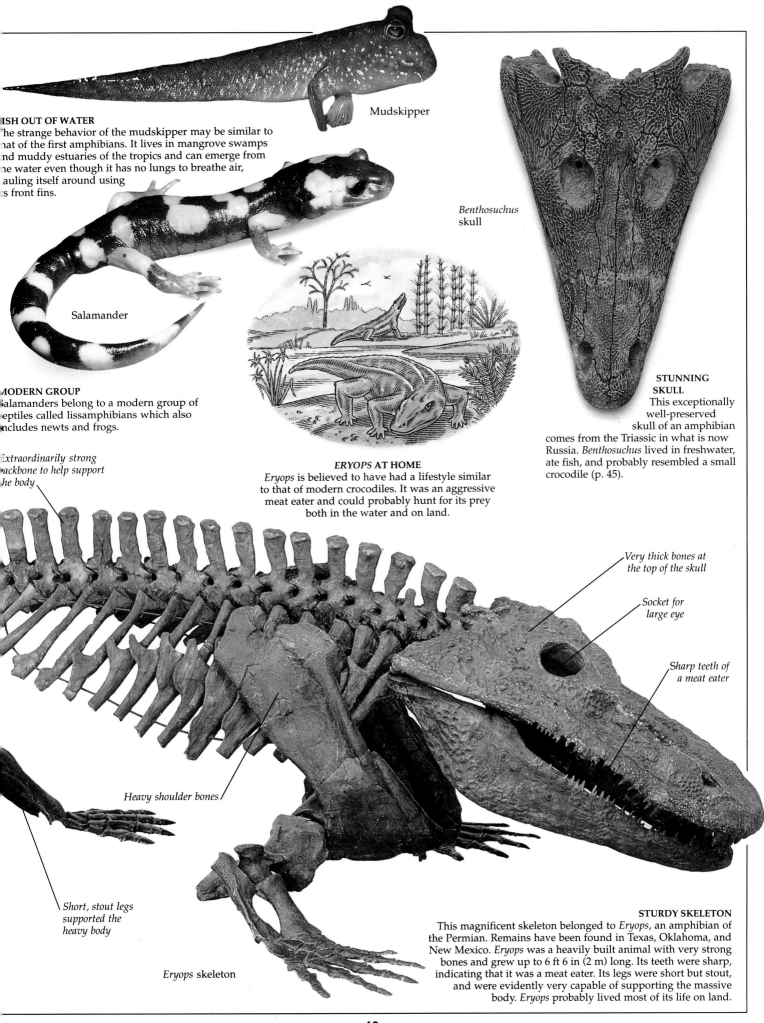

Mudskipper

FISH OUT OF WATER
The strange behavior of the mudskipper may be similar to
that of the first amphibians. It lives in mangrove swamps
and muddy estuaries of the tropics and can emerge from
the water even though it has no lungs to breathe air,
hauling itself around using
its front fins.

Salamander

MODERN GROUP
Salamanders belong to a modern group of
reptiles called lissamphibians which also
includes newts and frogs.

*Extraordinarily strong
backbone to help support
the body*

Benthosuchus
skull

STUNNING
SKULL
This exceptionally
well-preserved
skull of an amphibian
comes from the Triassic in what is now
Russia. *Benthosuchus* lived in freshwater,
ate fish, and probably resembled a small
crocodile (p. 45).

ERYOPS AT HOME
Eryops is believed to have had a lifestyle similar
to that of modern crocodiles. It was an aggressive
meat eater and could probably hunt for its prey
both in the water and on land.

*Very thick bones at
the top of the skull*

*Socket for
large eye*

*Sharp teeth of
a meat eater*

Heavy shoulder bones

*Short, stout legs
supported the
heavy body*

Eryops skeleton

STURDY SKELETON
This magnificent skeleton belonged to *Eryops*, an amphibian of
the Permian. Remains have been found in Texas, Oklahoma, and
New Mexico. *Eryops* was a heavily built animal with very strong
bones and grew up to 6 ft 6 in (2 m) long. Its teeth were sharp,
indicating that it was a meat eater. Its legs were short but stout,
and were evidently very capable of supporting the massive
body. *Eryops* probably lived most of its life on land.

Onto the land

THREE MAIN KINDS OF REPTILES live today: lizards and snakes, tortoises and turtles, and crocodiles. A fourth is represented only by the tuatara (p. 60). The number of surviving reptiles is much less than the number of extinct forms, especially those which lived in Mesozoic times such as dinosaurs (pp. 48–51), pterosaurs (p. 52), and ichthyosaurs and plesiosaurs (pp. 46–47). The first reptile fossils are found in rocks from the early Carboniferous, about 300 million years old. It is thought that these early reptiles possessed two important features, still seen in modern species, that enabled them to live away from water unlike amphibians: a special kind of egg, known as an amniote egg (below), and a scaly skin which protected their bodies against drying out.

There are over 2,000 species of snakes living today

BURIED EGGS
Sea-going turtles return to land to lay their eggs, which they bury in the warm sands of tropical beaches, and then return to the sea. The largest living turtle is the leatherback, which may reach 8 ft (2.5 m) in length. The Cretaceous turtle *Archelon* grew to more than 13 ft (4 m) long!

BODY GUARD
Trionyx is a turtle from the Eocene. Only the protective carapace, or shell, is preserved here – the bones are missing. The first turtles appeared in the Triassic and probably lacked the ability of modern species to withdraw their head, limbs, and tail completely. Another difference is that they had teeth, which are replaced in modern species by a sharp horny beak for slicing vegetation or meat.

Modern ladder snake

READY FOR LAND
Turtle eggs contain liquid and are protected by leathery shells. Before birth an embryo can develop through early stages into an animal able to breathe and live on land.

LEGLESS VERTEBRATE
The earliest fossil snakes come from the late Cretaceous. Snakes have a poor fossil record but vertebrae are occasionally found. These vertebrae of *Paleophis*, from the Paleocene of Mali, West Africa, were found separately but have been assembled to give an impression of one snake's backbone. Snakes probably evolved from a lizard-like ancestor, with their limbs getting smaller and smaller and eventually disappearing altogether. This is thought to have been the result of the animal adopting a burrowing lifestyle, which was later abandoned by true snakes. Two important features seen in modern snakes are the poisonous fangs, used to inject venom into prey, and the loosely connected skull bones, which enable the snake to open its mouth very wide to swallow large prey.

Sprawler

Semi-improved

Fully improved

GRADUAL IMPROVEMENT
The limb positions of reptiles gradually improved to support the weight of the body more efficiently. The different postures can still be seen today. Lizards are "sprawlers"; crocodiles have a "semi-improved" posture and are able to lift their bellies off the ground to move in a hurry. "Fully improved" animals include all the dinosaurs and also advanced mammals.

Flattened skull

Long body

Scaly skin prevents drying out

Powerful jaws

BABY PREDATOR
Crocodiles have changed little in appearance since the Jurassic – they all have long bodies, short legs, a flattened skull, and sharp teeth. Crocodiles (including alligators and gavials) are predators which swim slowly toward their prey before making a rapid grab with their powerful jaws.

Diplocynodon skull

CROCODILE HEAD
The largest fossil crocodile, *Deinosuchus*, from the Cretaceous of Texas, is estimated to have been 40–50 ft (12–15 m) long! This head belonged to an Oligocene crocodile, *Diplocynodon*.

Diagrams of a modern lizard

LONG LIZARD *right*
Because lizards generally live in dry, upland areas where the likelihood of burial is low, fossil examples are seldom found. The earliest examples are from the Triassic, and they were probably present in great numbers during the reign of their larger relatives the dinosaurs. This fossil lizard, *Adriosaurus*, had a very long body and is almost snakelike. Others had skin stretched between extended ribs so they were evidently able to glide through the air, like the modern "flying dragon" *Draco volans*, found in the East Indies.

Sea dragons

DURING MESOZOIC TIMES, when dinosaurs roamed the land, the seas were inhabited by several kinds of giant reptiles popularly known as sea dragons. The most numerous of these were the ichthyosaurs and plesiosaurs; a third group, the mosasaurs, became common toward the end of the Mesozoic. None of these marine reptiles was really a dragon, of course, but their remains may have contributed to the legends of the long-necked, fire-breathing monsters. Their ways of life were similar to modern marine mammals such as small whales, dolphins, and seals. Some were fish eaters; others ate belemnites (p. 29) and other mollusks (pp. 26–29). They all breathed air and were therefore forced to surface regularly. Ichthyosaurs, plesiosaurs, and mosasaurs all became extinct, as did the dinosaurs, about 65 million years ago at the end of the Cretaceous.

MARY ANNING
Mary Anning (1799–1847) is famous for the fossils she collected close to her home in Lyme Regis on the south coast of England. The cliffs here contain abundant fossils of animals which lived in the sea in Jurassic times. Between 1810 and 1812 Mary and her brother excavated a complete ichthyosaur (at the time thought to be a crocodile) which they sold for £23, a large sum of money in those days.

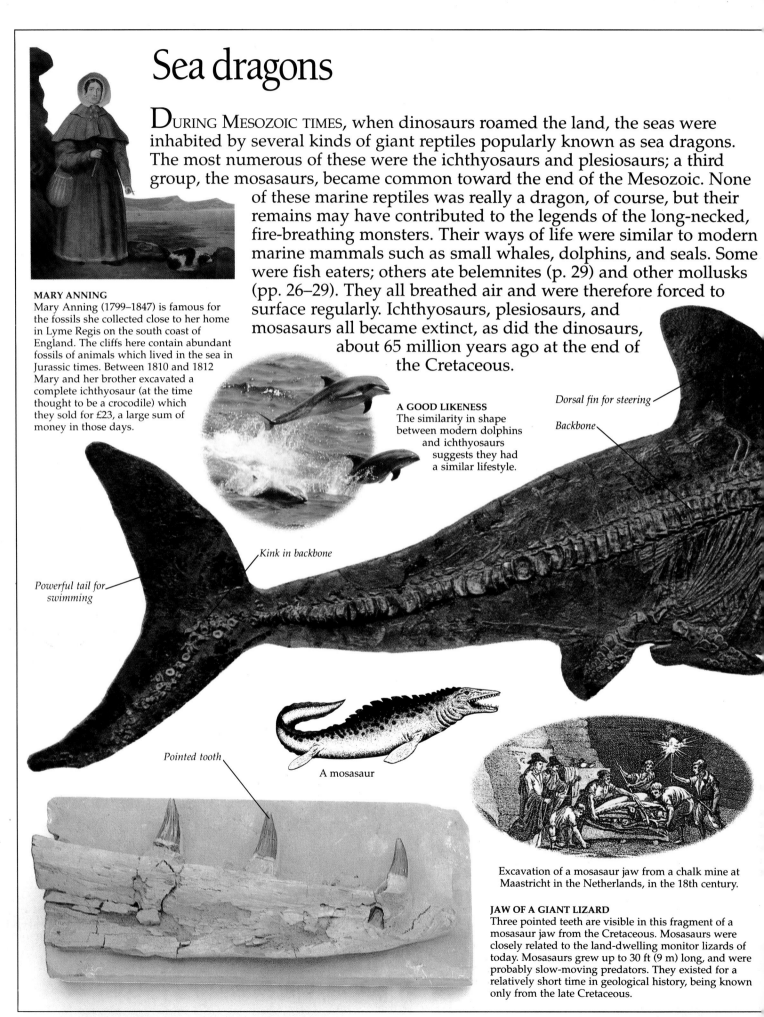

A GOOD LIKENESS
The similarity in shape between modern dolphins and ichthyosaurs suggests they had a similar lifestyle.

Dorsal fin for steering

Backbone

Kink in backbone

Powerful tail for swimming

Pointed tooth

A mosasaur

Excavation of a mosasaur jaw from a chalk mine at Maastricht in the Netherlands, in the 18th century.

JAW OF A GIANT LIZARD
Three pointed teeth are visible in this fragment of a mosasaur jaw from the Cretaceous. Mosasaurs were closely related to the land-dwelling monitor lizards of today. Mosasaurs grew up to 30 ft (9 m) long, and were probably slow-moving predators. They existed for a relatively short time in geological history, being known only from the late Cretaceous.

Ring of bones around eye socket

Short, sharp teeth

SAMUEL CLARKE
Samuel Clarke (1815–1898) was an amateur geologist who lived near Lyme Regis. He knew the area well and directed professionals to the most likely spots for finding sea dragons. He is holding the skull of a plesiosaur found in 1863.

PACKED TEETH
The long jaws of most ichthyosaurs are crammed with short, sharp teeth. Ichthyosaurs had large eyes, and it is thought that the ring of bones around the eye sockets improved their focusing ability. Their nostrils were far back on the top of the skull, as in modern dolphins and whales. This made it easier for the animals to breathe when they surfaced for air.

BATTLE OF THE SEA DRAGONS
A fictitious encounter between an ichthyosaur and a long-necked plesiosaur.

Outline of soft tissue

Neck vertebrae close together

Long jaws

Eye socket

Packed teeth

Paddle for steering

STREAMLINED PREDATOR
The streamlined shape of an ichthyosaur is seen in this fine Jurassic specimen in which an outline of the soft tissues has been preserved as well as the skeleton. The neck vertebrae of ichthyosaurs were close together so that the head ran smoothly into the body. This is typical of fast-swimming predators and is also seen in dolphins today. Ichthyosaurs swam by moving their powerful tails. Their backbones had a downward kink, as they extended only into the lower part of the tail fin. When the first skeletons were discovered, it was thought that these backbones were broken tails. The dorsal fin and paddles were used for steering and stability. Unlike most reptiles, ichthyosaurs gave birth to live young. Some specimens have been found with young inside the body cavity of adults, and several examples are known of mothers fossilized in the act of giving birth.

PADDLE POWER
The limbs of plesiosaurs formed large paddles. Like a turtle, a plesiosaur probably flapped these up and down when swimming.

TIME OF THE ICHTHYOSAURS
Dating back to the Triassic, ichthyosaurs were especially common in the Jurassic and survived into the late Cretaceous.

Fossil giants

Dinosaurs are probably the most impressive of all fossils. There were many different species, and their reign spanned 150 million years from the Triassic to the end of the Cretaceous. Dinosaurs were reptiles. Not all of them were huge; there were large ones and small ones. Some were plant-eaters, others were meat-eaters. Some had armored plates, others had spiked or clubbed tails. The variety was enormous. We know about dinosaurs from their skeletons, and detailed restorations of them can be made from their bones (p. 14). We cannot know for certain what color they were, but we can make a guess based on the color of reptiles living today. The mysterious extinction of the dinosaurs at the end of Cretaceous times has stimulated many different theories, such as a change in climate or a meteor impact. The dinosaurs did not all die out at once. By the end of the Cretaceous, they were already reduced from hundreds of species to fewer than twenty.

FOOD GRINDER
Apatosaurus, a large Jurassic sauropod, weighed about 30 tons. Like all sauropods, it was a plant eater, probably using its long neck to reach leaves on trees. Its teeth were relatively small, and it is thought that *Apatosaurus* swallowed stones which then acted as a mill, grinding up the food in its stomach. Modern crocodiles use stones in a similar way.

MONSTER-STALKING
Although all the giant Mesozoic reptiles became extinct long before humans appeared, some people still search for living examples of these monsters.

Edmontosaurus

PLANT EATER
One of the last-surviving dinosaurs was *Edmontosaurus*. It was a hadrosaur, or duckbill, which grew to about 43 ft (13 m) long. Hadrosaurs were once thought to live partly in water, feeding on water plants, but land-plant fossils have been found with some skeletons, which suggests that a diet of trees and shrubs was more likely. These were dealt with by powerful teeth – about 1,000 in *Edmontosaurus*. Hadrosaurs laid their eggs in mound-shaped nests. A colony of closely grouped hadrosaur nests was discovered in Montana, indicating that the animals may have lived in herds. The nests had young of different ages in them so the adults apparently protected their young.

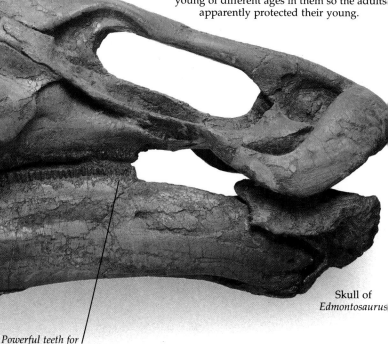

Powerful teeth for crushing leaves

Skull of
Edmontosaurus

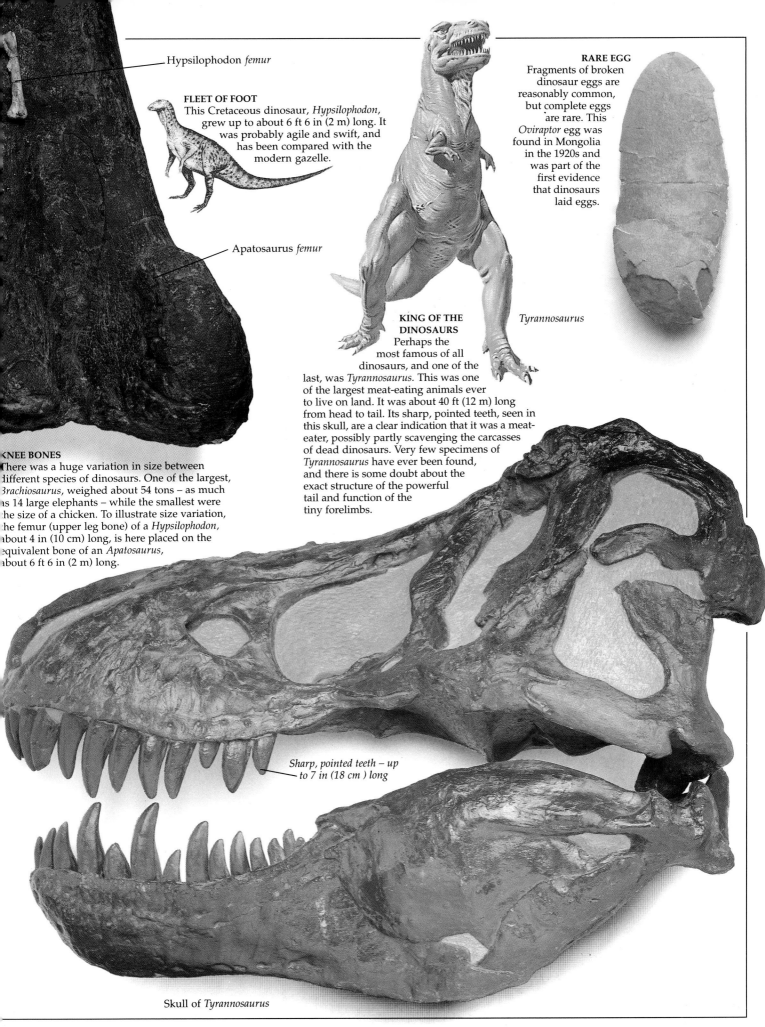

Hypsilophodon *femur*

FLEET OF FOOT
This Cretaceous dinosaur, *Hypsilophodon*,
grew up to about 6 ft 6 in (2 m) long. It
was probably agile and swift, and
has been compared with the
modern gazelle.

RARE EGG
Fragments of broken
dinosaur eggs are
reasonably common,
but complete eggs
are rare. This
Oviraptor egg was
found in Mongolia
in the 1920s and
was part of the
first evidence
that dinosaurs
laid eggs.

Apatosaurus *femur*

Tyrannosaurus

**KING OF THE
DINOSAURS**
Perhaps the
most famous of all
dinosaurs, and one of the
last, was *Tyrannosaurus*. This was one
of the largest meat-eating animals ever
to live on land. It was about 40 ft (12 m) long
from head to tail. Its sharp, pointed teeth, seen in
this skull, are a clear indication that it was a meat-
eater, possibly partly scavenging the carcasses
of dead dinosaurs. Very few specimens of
Tyrannosaurus have ever been found,
and there is some doubt about the
exact structure of the powerful
tail and function of the
tiny forelimbs.

KNEE BONES
There was a huge variation in size between
different species of dinosaurs. One of the largest,
Brachiosaurus, weighed about 54 tons – as much
as 14 large elephants – while the smallest were
the size of a chicken. To illustrate size variation,
the femur (upper leg bone) of a *Hypsilophodon*,
about 4 in (10 cm) long, is here placed on the
equivalent bone of an *Apatosaurus*,
about 6 ft 6 in (2 m) long.

*Sharp, pointed teeth – up
to 7 in (18 cm) long*

Skull of *Tyrannosaurus*

Discovering dinosaurs

Iguanodon tooth

THE FIRST DESCRIPTIONS of the fossil bones of dinosaurs were made over 150 years ago. First some teeth, and then some bones of *Iguanodon* were found in southern England by an English doctor, Gideon Mantell, and his wife. Later, bones of the dinosaurs *Megalosaurus* and *Hylaeosaurus* were also discovered. In 1841, Richard Owen, a leading British anatomist, invented the name "dinosaur," which means "terrible lizard," for these early discoveries. They were followed by many more all around the world. Huge numbers of dinosaur remains were found in North America during the second half of the 19th century and into the 20th century, and other significant finds were made in Tanzania, China, Mongolia, and Argentina. Important dinosaur discoveries are still being made, of species already known and of new species. Almost every new discovery adds to our knowledge of these magnificent extinct reptiles.

CLAWS DISCOVERER
Bill Walker holding the claw bone of *Baryonyx* which he discovered in 1983.

MANTELL'S TOOTH!
This is one of the original *Iguanodon* teeth which were named by Mantell in 1825.

MANTELL'S QUARRY
Mantell was a doctor of medicine and an enthusiastic collector of fossils. The *Iguanodon* teeth and bones he described came from an old quarry in the Cuckfield area of southern England. Here rocks of early Cretaceous age were dug for use as gravel.

BIG REPTILE
In 1824, William Buckland discovered some dinosaur bones in Stonesfield in Oxfordshire, England. He gave the animal the name *Megalosaurus*, which means "big reptile." Buckland was a teacher of geology at the University of Oxford when he described his dinosaur. This jawbone belonged to a *Megalosaurus* and comes from the same area as Buckland's specimens.

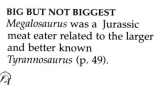

BIG BUT NOT BIGGEST
Megalosaurus was a Jurassic meat eater related to the larger and better known *Tyrannosaurus* (p. 49).

EDWARD DRINKER COPE
Between 1870 and 1897 Cope took part in what has been described as the great dinosaur gold rush. It took place in the U.S., primarily in the states of Montana and Wyoming. Two names are especially associated with this gold rush - Cope and Marsh. Each hired independent teams of collectors to excavate dinosaur bones in the race to be first to describe the many new species.

OTHNIEL CHARLES MARSH
In this cartoon, Marsh is depicted as a circus ringmaster leading his team of prehistoric animals. The intense rivalry between Cope and Marsh caused the two men to swap a succession of insults, and even to destroy incomplete fossils in their own quarries in order to prevent future collection by their rival!

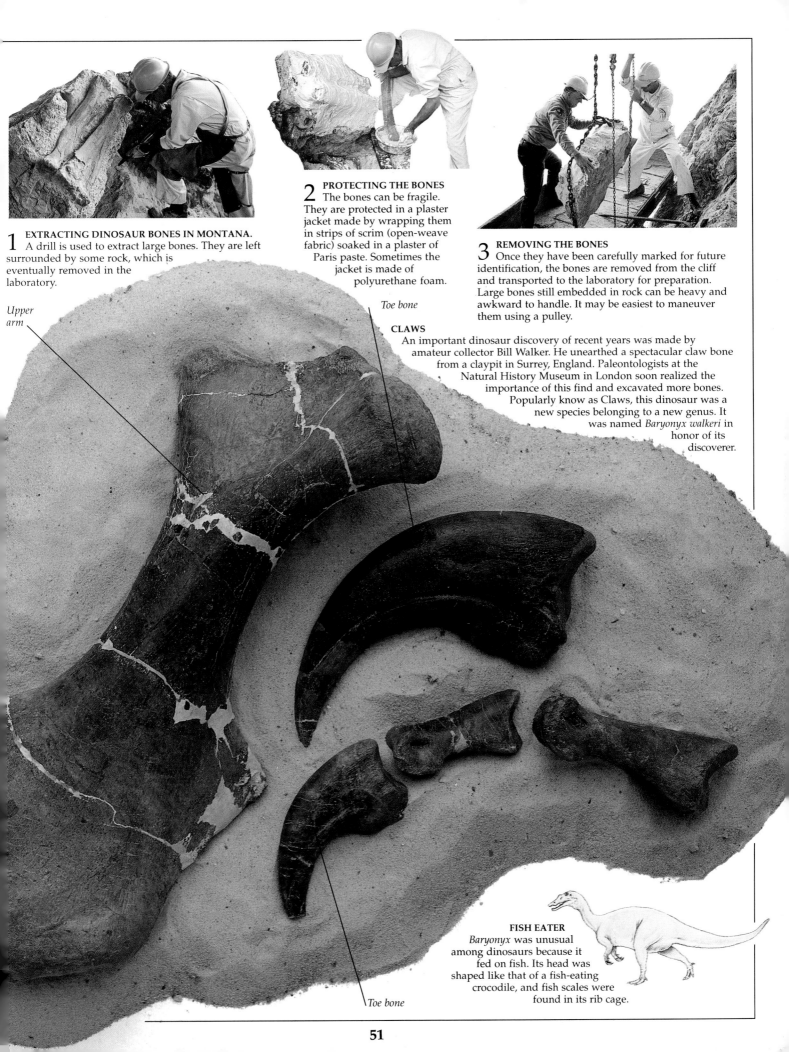

1 **EXTRACTING DINOSAUR BONES IN MONTANA.**
A drill is used to extract large bones. They are left surrounded by some rock, which is eventually removed in the laboratory.

2 **PROTECTING THE BONES**
The bones can be fragile. They are protected in a plaster jacket made by wrapping them in strips of scrim (open-weave fabric) soaked in a plaster of Paris paste. Sometimes the jacket is made of polyurethane foam.

3 **REMOVING THE BONES**
Once they have been carefully marked for future identification, the bones are removed from the cliff and transported to the laboratory for preparation. Large bones still embedded in rock can be heavy and awkward to handle. It may be easiest to maneuver them using a pulley.

CLAWS
An important dinosaur discovery of recent years was made by amateur collector Bill Walker. He unearthed a spectacular claw bone from a claypit in Surrey, England. Paleontologists at the Natural History Museum in London soon realized the importance of this find and excavated more bones. Popularly know as Claws, this dinosaur was a new species belonging to a new genus. It was named *Baryonyx walkeri* in honor of its discoverer.

Upper arm

Toe bone

FISH EATER
Baryonyx was unusual among dinosaurs because it fed on fish. Its head was shaped like that of a fish-eating crocodile, and fish scales were found in its rib cage.

Toe bone

Winged wonders

THE FIRST ANIMALS TO FLY were insects; fossil dragonflies have been found in rocks more than 300 million years old. Flying vertebrates appeared almost 100 million years later. True flapping flight has evolved in three groups of vertebrates: pterosaurs (extinct), bats, and birds. They are not closely related, and their ability to fly has evolved independently. Pterosaurs were reptiles, related to dinosaurs (pp. 48–51), with a greatly lengthened fourth finger. This supported the fleshy membrane, a thin sheet of muscle and elastic fibers covered by skin, which was the wing. In birds, the feathered wing is supported by several fingers and the lower part of the forearm. Bats are flying mammals and have wings made of a fleshy membrane similar to that of pterosaurs but supported by four fingers. Because bones of flying vertebrates have to be light, they are fragile and are seldom fossilized.

WING SUPPORT
This is one of the long finger bones which supported the wing of a *Pteranodon*, one of the largest flying animals that ever lived. The wingspan of this Cretaceous pterosaur was about 23 ft (7 m).

WELL-BALANCED
Pteranodon was a pterosaur with a bony crest on its head which counterbalanced its long toothless beak. It appears to have been a fish eater which soared over the oceans like the modern albatross.

IMAGINARY BIRD
The finding of pterosaur remains fueled the imagination of authors of science fiction stories.

FURRY REPTILE
The small Jurassic pterosaur *Pterodactylus* had membranous wings, claws, a toothed beak, and a body covered by fine fur. Evidence for fur comes from some pterosaurs that were discovered in Kazakhstan with hairlike impressions around the body. This may indicate that pterosaurs were warm-blooded and used the fur as insulation. The tail of *Pterodactylus* was short, and it had a wing span of only about 20 in (50 cm), but some pterosaurs – including *Rhamphorhynchus*, with a wingspan of 5 ft (1.5 m) – had long tails. Pterosaurs first appeared during the Triassic and became extinct at the end of the Cretaceous.

Toothed beak

Greatly lengthened fourth finger

Membranous wing

Short tail

Body covered by fine fur

Claws

MISTAKEN IDENTITY
This small dinosaur belongs to a group which many scientists believe were ancestors of birds. In 1973, some museum paleontologists in German realized that one of their specimens, long identified as *Compsognathus*, was really an *Archaeopteryx*!

FLYING MAMMAL
It is easy to see the similarity between this bat and the pterosaurs. Bats date from the Eocene. Because bats often roost in caves, their fossil bones can be found in large numbers in cave deposits.

Impression of feathers like a bird's

Clawed fingers like a reptile's

Teeth unlike a modern bird

Archaeopteryx had a wingspan of about 20 in (50 cm)

Fossil feather

Modern bird's feather

RARE FIND
Feathers occur only in birds and are seldom fossilized. Very occasionally they are found in fine-grained sediments such as this Oligocene limestone.

THE FIRST BIRD
Archaeopteryx lived 150 million years ago. Specimens of it, all found in Germany, are generally regarded as the most precious fossils in the world. Only five more have been discovered since this first one, found in 1861 and now in the Museum of Natural History in East Berlin. *Archaeopteryx* was intermediate between reptiles and birds. Some specimens show clear feather impressions.

Bony tail like a reptile's

Claws

Ostrich

ELEPHANTINE EGG
The Madagascan elephant bird, *Aepyornis maximus*, stood over 6 ft 6 in (2 m) high. Its fossil eggs are the largest birds' eggs known, reaching 35 in (90 cm) in circumference. One is compared here with an ostrich egg, one of the largest modern birds' eggs, to show how enormous it really is.

Ostrich egg

Elephant bird egg

FINE SKULL
Fossilized remains of birds are rare. This finely preserved Eocene skull comes from the bird *Prophaethon*. Some scientists think that *Prophaethon* was a close relative of the tropic bird *Phaethon*.

Modern tropic bird

Elephant bird

Mammal variety

ANIMALS AS VARIED AS MICE, ELEPHANTS, kangaroos, bats, cats, whales, horses, and humans are all mammals. They are warm-blooded and produce milk to suckle their infants. Most give birth to live young, have hairy skin and complex teeth, and are highly active. A mammal whose babies develop inside the mother's womb, such as a cat, is known as a placental mammal. The babies of marsupial mammals (pp. 56–57), such as the kangaroo, develop inside the mother's pouch after birth. The first mammals appeared at about the same time as the earliest dinosaurs, 200 million years ago. Nearly all Mesozoic mammals were small shrew-like animals, but in the Cenozoic they diversified into the many different types we are familiar with today. Complete fossil mammals are rare; many species are known only from their teeth. Nevertheless, from these it is possible to build up a picture of the variety of species, what they ate, and the way they lived.

Chisel-like incisor teeth

Skull of *Ischyromys*

Berries

RODENTS
Rodents include rats, mice, and squirrels, and are among the most diverse of mammals. Their large chisel-like incisor teeth grow continuously during life and are used to gnaw a variety of foods. Rodents date from Paleocene times. This example is *Ischyromys* from the famous Oligocene mammal beds of the Badlands in South Dakota.

Modern squirrel

Ants

Skull of *Orycteropus*

INSECT EATERS
Insect-eating mammals are generally small and include shrews and moles. *Orycteropus* was a Miocene aardvark, a peculiar kind of anteater. Mammals living on a diet of ants have several features in common, including a long hard palate in the roof of the mouth which helps prevent ants from entering the windpipe.

Modern aardvark

ICE AGE MAMMAL
Mammoths were elephant-like mammals adapted to life in cold climates during the Pleistocene Ice Ages. Some skeletons have been found preserved in the frozen ground of Siberia (p. 20).

High-crowned cheek teeth

Modern camel

Skull of *Cainotherium*

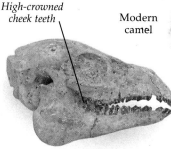

PLANT EATERS
Many herbivorous mammals, which feed on vegetation, have cheek teeth with high crowns capable of withstanding wear caused by constant chewing. They can be divided into browsers, which eat mostly leaves, and grazers, which eat mostly grass. This skull belonged to *Cainotherium*, a rabbit-like browser whose closest, but very distant, living relative is probably the camel.

Ridges of hard enamel

GRINDING TOOTH
Mammoths were enormous and needed to eat large quantities of vegetation. Their huge high-crowned cheek teeth had ridges of hard enamel on the grinding surface. This enabled them to grind up vegetation with great efficiency.

Leaves

Skull of *Proconsul*

FRUIT EATERS
Monkeys, apes, and humans belong to a group of mammals called the primates. Many primates are omnivores (*omni* means "all") and have a mixed diet, but some eat mostly fruit. Shown here is the skull of the Miocene ape *Proconsul*. The blunt teeth are typical of fruit eaters. As fruit is poor in protein, *Proconsul* may have supplemented its diet with leaves from the trees in which it lived.

Modern monkey

Blunt teeth typical of a fruit eater

Fruit

Nuts

EOCENE LANDSCAPE
Mammals first became common in the Eocene. Many of the mammals which roamed the land belonged to groups with no living descendants.

Skull of *Hoplophoneus*

Large canine tooth

Meat

MEAT EATERS
Carnivorous or meat-eating mammals have large canine teeth. These were developed to their greatest extent in the upper jaws of the so-called sabertooths. They may have used their long teeth to stab the necks of their prey. This skull belongs to *Hoplophoneus* from the Oligocene. Unfortunately, none of the several different sorts of sabertooth known from the fossil record have survived to the present day.

Sabertooth cat

Canine tooth

Skull of *Potamotherium*

FISH EATERS
Potamotherium lived in freshwater lakes during the early Miocene and fed on fish. It was similar to a modern otter but was better adapted to life in water than otters. It may have been a forerunner of seals, which first became common in the sea during the late Miocene.

Fish

Modern otters

A boxing kangaroo

A world apart

AUSTRALIA IS AN ISLAND CONTINENT. The geological record shows that it has been isolated for 50 million years, ever since plate movements (pp. 12–13) caused the continent to drift away from Antarctica. This is the reason why many of the native mammals in Australia are unique. Marsupials differ from other mammals in having pouches in which the young are reared for a period after birth. The fleshy pouches do not fossilize, but there are features of the bones and teeth that distinguish fossils of marsupials from those of placentals (pp. 54–55). Marsupials evolved on their own, away from the placental mammals that came to dominate them in other parts of the world. Fossils of many extinct marsupials have been found, including *Diprotodon*, the centerpiece of these pages. There are still many species of pouched mammals in Australia, including the kangaroo and koala. Other native mammals unique to the country include the extraordinary egg-laying monotremes – the platypus and the echidna.

Hip bone connecting the leg to the spine

TWO FRONT TEETH
This magnificent skeleton of the extinct marsupial *Diprotodon* is about 10 ft (3 m) long. Its name, meaning "two front teeth, refers to the large, rodentlike incisors that were used for cropping vegetation. Note the pair of epipubic bones in the pelvic area, which can be used to distinguish pouched from placental mammals. *Diprotodon* comes from Pleistocene rocks and many skeletons have been excavated from Lake Callabonna, a dried-up lake in South Australia. It is possible that *Diprotodon* survived until more recent times and was hunted by early Australians – some animals in ancient Aboriginal paintings could be *Diprotodon*.

Epipubic bones that helped support the pouch

Tail vertebrae

60 million years ago

Australia

Antarctica

45 million years ago

Australia

Antarctica

DRIFTING CONTINENTS
These two maps show the position of Australia about 60 million years ago (top) and 45 million years ago (bottom) after the split from Antarctica. The isolation of Australia prevented its colonization by placental mammals, apart from some bats and rodents. These might otherwise have replaced the native animals. This is probably what happened to the marsupials of South America, such as the extinct sabertooth *Thylacosmilus*, when placental mammals invaded South America after North and South America joined.

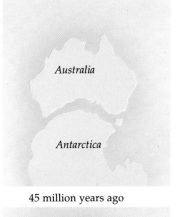

GIANT WOMBAT?
Diprotodon (above) was a herbivore. It probably looked like a long-legged wombat (opposite).

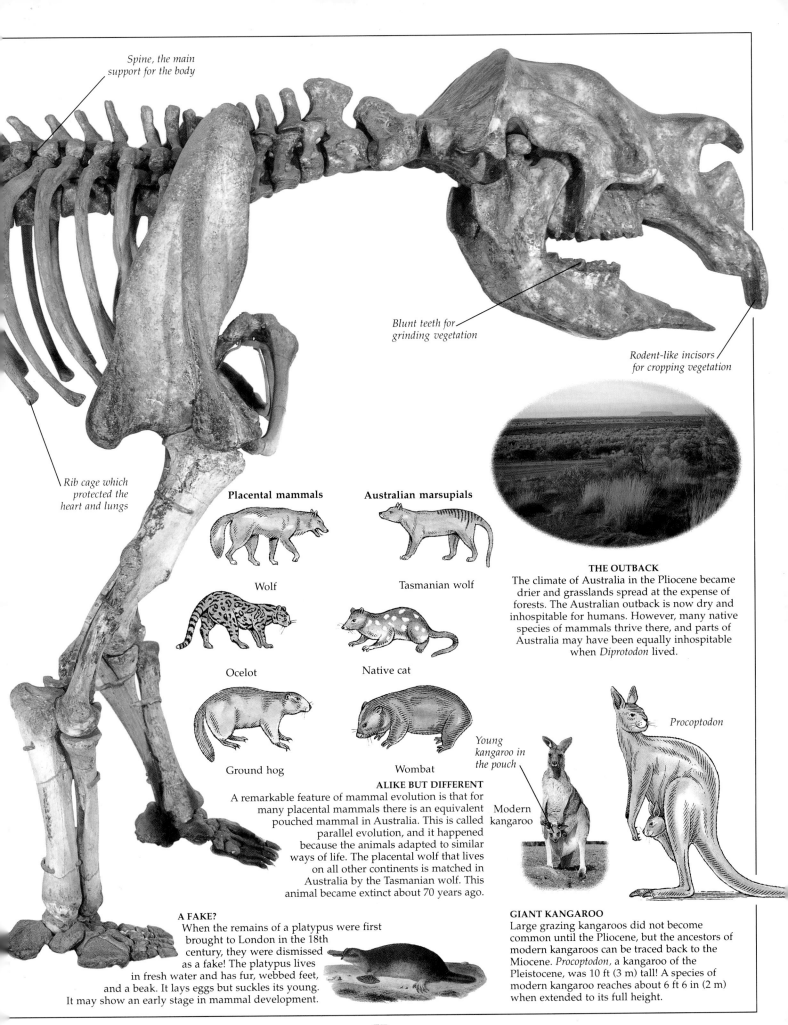

Spine, the main support for the body

Blunt teeth for grinding vegetation

Rodent-like incisors for cropping vegetation

Rib cage which protected the heart and lungs

Placental mammals

Wolf

Ocelot

Ground hog

Australian marsupials

Tasmanian wolf

Native cat

Wombat

THE OUTBACK
The climate of Australia in the Pliocene became drier and grasslands spread at the expense of forests. The Australian outback is now dry and inhospitable for humans. However, many native species of mammals thrive there, and parts of Australia may have been equally inhospitable when *Diprotodon* lived.

Procoptodon

Young kangaroo in the pouch

Modern kangaroo

ALIKE BUT DIFFERENT
A remarkable feature of mammal evolution is that for many placental mammals there is an equivalent pouched mammal in Australia. This is called parallel evolution, and it happened because the animals adapted to similar ways of life. The placental wolf that lives on all other continents is matched in Australia by the Tasmanian wolf. This animal became extinct about 70 years ago.

A FAKE?
When the remains of a platypus were first brought to London in the 18th century, they were dismissed as a fake! The platypus lives in fresh water and has fur, webbed feet, and a beak. It lays eggs but suckles its young. It may show an early stage in mammal development.

GIANT KANGAROO
Large grazing kangaroos did not become common until the Pliocene, but the ancestors of modern kangaroos can be traced back to the Miocene. *Procoptodon*, a kangaroo of the Pleistocene, was 10 ft (3 m) tall! A species of modern kangaroo reaches about 6 ft 6 in (2 m) when extended to its full height.

Human fossils

FOSSILS OF PEOPLE (hominids) are rare and fragmentary, but have been found in increasing numbers during the past few years. They tell us a great deal about the origin and development of modern people. The story begins with the apelike *Ardipithecus* and *Australopithecus* and ends with *Homo sapiens.* The nearest living relatives of humans are the African great apes (chimpanzees and gorillas), but there are many differences between us and them. These include a larger brain in humans and the ability to walk on two legs rather than four. Study of fossil hominids shows how these differences developed through geological time. Typical human features first appeared in *Australopithecus*, distinguishing them from their even more apelike ancestors.

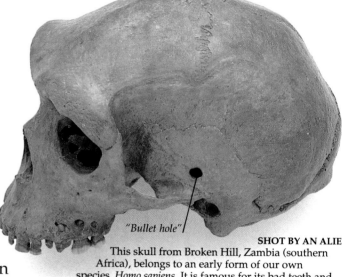

"Bullet hole"

SHOT BY AN ALIEN?
This skull from Broken Hill, Zambia (southern Africa), belongs to an early form of our own species, *Homo sapiens*. It is famous for its bad teeth and the hole in one side. An imaginative writer interpreted this as a hole made by a bullet shot by a visitor from another planet 120,000 years ago! In fact it is a partly healed abscess.

Adult's footprint

Child's footprint

FIRST STEPS
At some stage in human evolution, bipedalism (standing upright and walking on two legs) developed. These footprints from Tanzania (East Africa) were made by two-footed hominids 3.6 million years ago. They were probably two adults and a child *Australopithecus* who walked across a surface of damp volcanic ash. The ash hardened and was buried beneath more ash and sediment. The fossil footprints were discovered by a team led by Mary Leakey in 1977. They prove that a species of primate walked on two feet at least 3.6 million years ago. This ties in with evidence from fossil bones that *Australopithecus* walked on two legs.

Chimpanzee skull

Human skull

COMPARING FEATURES
These skulls of a modern human and an ape – a chimpanzee – look very similar, but careful comparison shows some of the differences. Humans have much larger brains than chimps. The average volume of a human's brain is 1,400 cc; a chimp's brain is about 400 cc. This is reflected in the domed human cranium, necessary to house the large brain, compared with the low chimp cranium. Another obvious difference is the flatter muzzle of the human. The teeth are also different. For example, a chimp cannot move its jaws from side to side so much when it is chewing, because its canine teeth overlap.

Carved reindeer

ARTISTIC BEGINNINGS
This sculpted antler is over 12,000 years old and shows a male reindeer following a female reindeer. It was probably carved using simple flint tools and reveals a high quality of craftsmanship. Such art forms show the development of the cultural activities (art, literature, music, etc) which are unique to humans.

Using a stone to
chip off flakes

THE OLDEST TOOLS
The human being is often described as
the toolmaker. This pebble tool is one of
the oldest recognizable stone tools,
thought to have been made by
Homo habilis ("handy man")
almost 2 million years ago. The
flint handaxe is about
200,000 years old.
Both tools were made
by chipping off flakes
to sharpen them.

Pebble
tool

Flint handaxe

SOUTHERN APE
Several sorts of *Australopithecus*
("southern ape") lived in Africa
between about 5 and 1.5 million
years ago. Certain species were heavily
built and had bony crests on their skulls. Others
were lightly built, like this example from South
Africa. It is possible that these forms are direct
ancestors of modern humans.

LOUIS LEAKEY
The oldest hominids have been found in South
and East Africa. Among the paleontologists
responsible for their discovery have been the
Leakey family – the late Louis Leakey, his wife,
Mary, and their son, Richard.
Louis, pictured here, is
known especially for his
finds of *Australopithecus* at
Olduvai Gorge in Tanzania.

LUCY
This is the
skeleton of an
adult female
Australopithecus. It
was discovered in 1974 and
named after the Beatles' song
"Lucy in the Sky with Diamonds."

UPRIGHT MAN
Homo erectus ("upright man") has been found
not only in Africa but also in Southeast Asia.
They lived between about 1.6 million and 500,000
years ago. The size of the cranium indicates a brain size of about
1,000 cc, larger than *Australopithecus* but smaller than modern
humans. *Homo erectus* used fire. An example from China – Peking
Man – was found in a cave deposit with a fossilized hearth that was
used for either cooking
or providing heat
and light.

*Carved animal
head*

Harpoon

ROCK PAINTING
These paintings of animals
were done by early people
living in what is now
Algeria (Northwest Africa).

Sickle

Arrowheads

*Sharp
flint
pieces*

HUNTING TOOLS
These 4,000-year-old arrowheads are made
of flint, a rock favored by early people
because of the ease with which flakes could
be struck off to shape different tools. The
10,000-year-old sickle is made of goat horn
with sharp pieces of flint embedded to form
a cutting edge. The barbed harpoon was
carved from an antler.

ICE-AGE RELATIVE
Neanderthals lived in Europe and western Asia
before and during the last Ice Age, between 100,000
and 35,000 years ago. They were given the name because the first specimen to be
described was found in a cave in the Neander valley, Germany. They used to be
thought of as a subspecies of *Homo sapiens* ("thinking man"); today they are classed
as a species alone, *Homo neanderthalensis*. The brutish caveman image often given to
Neanderthals is incorrect. On average, their brains were larger than our own. They
were also shorter, stocky, and relatively hairy – well adapted to life in cold climates.

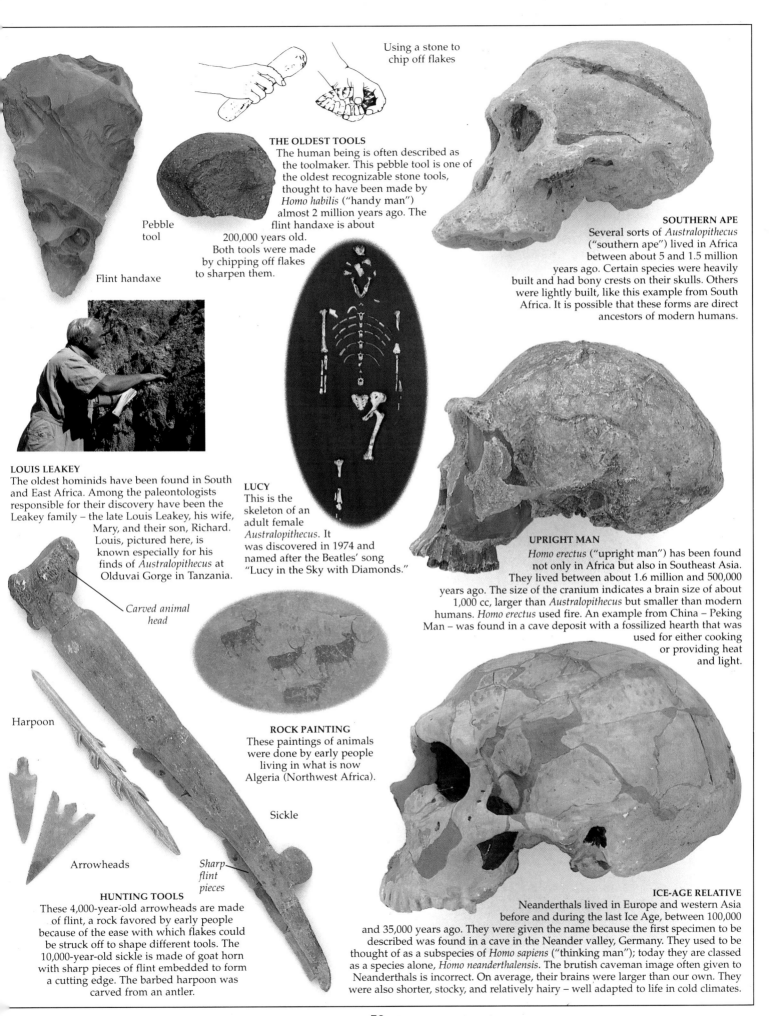

Living fossils

FOSSILS SHOW US that animals and plants have changed enormously since life on Earth began. Some have changed so much that modern species are very different from their fossil ancestors. At the other extreme, there are animals and plants living today that are almost identical to fossils millions of years old. The most striking examples of these "living fossils" are those animals and plants which are rare nowadays, such as the coelacanth and slit shells, which were known as fossils before they were discovered to be still living. Among plant species which have survived up to the present day are the horsetail (pp. 36–37) from the Devonian, the monkey-puzzle tree (pp. 36–37) and the ginkgo from the Triassic, and the magnolia, one of the earliest true flowering plants, from the Cretaceous.

LAST SURVIVOR
The tuatara is the only living survivor of a group of reptiles that were abundant during Triassic times. It looks like a lizard but its skull has a different bone structure. The tuatara lives only on a few islands off New Zealand.

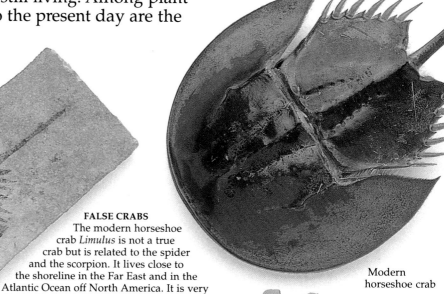

Fossil horseshoe crab

Modern horseshoe crab

FALSE CRABS
The modern horseshoe crab *Limulus* is not a true crab but is related to the spider and the scorpion. It lives close to the shoreline in the Far East and in the Atlantic Ocean off North America. It is very similar to the fossil *Mesolimulus*, an animal that lived in the sea about 150 million years ago. Other fossil horseshoe crabs include species that lived in freshwater swamps 300 million years ago.

Ginkgo *leaf*

ANCIENT INSECT
Still common today, cockroaches, together with dragonflies, are among the oldest of all insects and range back to the Carboniferous. Some fossil cockroaches closely resemble modern species.

Modern cockroaches

Fossil cockroach

Fan-shaped *leaves*

Fossil *Ginkgo*

LONE RANGER
Ginkgos first appeared in the Triassic and were much more wide-spread in the past than they are today. Only a single species, *Ginkgo biloba*, lives today. Ginkgos are hardy trees that grow naturally in the forests of western China but can also be seen in many cities around the world because they are not easily hurt by pollution. The characteristic fan-shaped leaves are easily recognizable when fossilized, as in this Jurassic example.

Modern *Ginkgo* branch

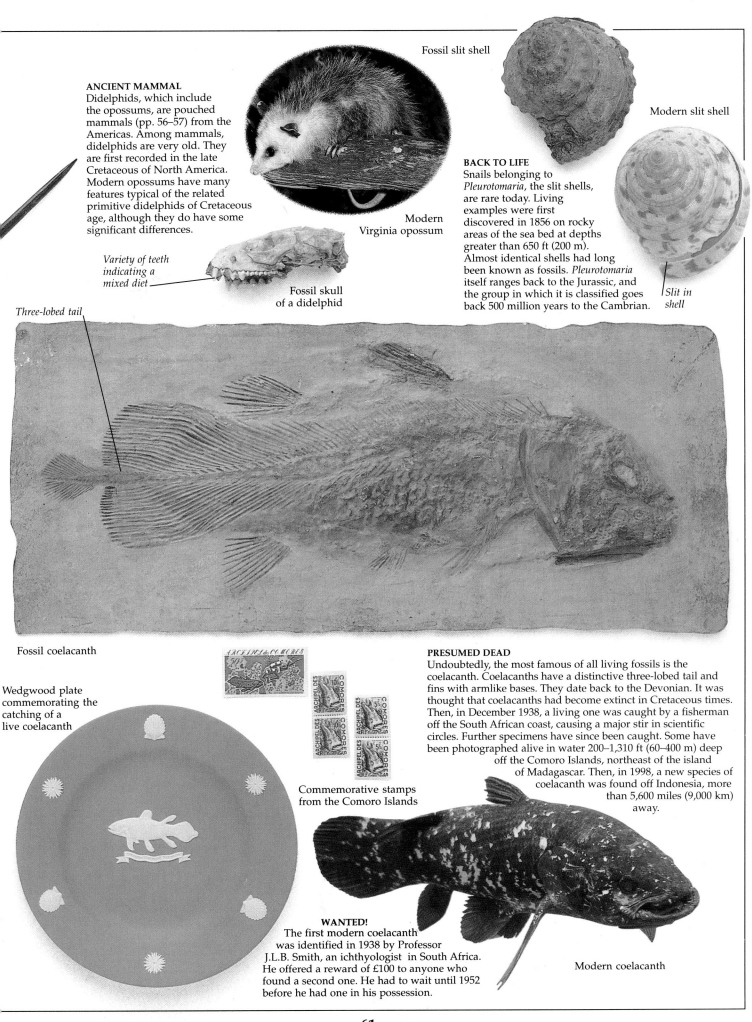

ANCIENT MAMMAL
Didelphids, which include the opossums, are pouched mammals (pp. 56–57) from the Americas. Among mammals, didelphids are very old. They are first recorded in the late Cretaceous of North America. Modern opossums have many features typical of the related primitive didelphids of Cretaceous age, although they do have some significant differences.

Fossil slit shell

Modern slit shell

Modern Virginia opossum

Variety of teeth indicating a mixed diet

Fossil skull of a didelphid

BACK TO LIFE
Snails belonging to *Pleurotomaria*, the slit shells, are rare today. Living examples were first discovered in 1856 on rocky areas of the sea bed at depths greater than 650 ft (200 m). Almost identical shells had long been known as fossils. *Pleurotomaria* itself ranges back to the Jurassic, and the group in which it is classified goes back 500 million years to the Cambrian.

Slit in shell

Three-lobed tail

Fossil coelacanth

Wedgwood plate commemorating the catching of a live coelacanth

Commemorative stamps from the Comoro Islands

PRESUMED DEAD
Undoubtedly, the most famous of all living fossils is the coelacanth. Coelacanths have a distinctive three-lobed tail and fins with armlike bases. They date back to the Devonian. It was thought that coelacanths had become extinct in Cretaceous times. Then, in December 1938, a living one was caught by a fisherman off the South African coast, causing a major stir in scientific circles. Further specimens have since been caught. Some have been photographed alive in water 200–1,310 ft (60–400 m) deep off the Comoro Islands, northeast of the island of Madagascar. Then, in 1998, a new species of coelacanth was found off Indonesia, more than 5,600 miles (9,000 km) away.

WANTED!
The first modern coelacanth was identified in 1938 by Professor J.L.B. Smith, an ichthyologist in South Africa. He offered a reward of £100 to anyone who found a second one. He had to wait until 1952 before he had one in his possession.

Modern coelacanth

Fossil hunting

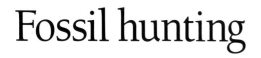

To FIND THE FOSSIL REMAINS of a creature that lived millions of years ago is a thrilling experience. Fossil collecting is a hobby that can be enjoyed by anyone using the most basic tools. Sea cliffs, quarries, and other exposures of rock all over the world provide productive places for fossil collectors but safety must always be kept in mind. It may be necessary to get permission to collect from landowners, and attention must be paid to conservation - fossil localities can easily be ruined by over-collecting.

An historic find?

FIELD NOTEBOOK
The type of rock formation and locality of finds should be recorded in a field notebook.

HAMMERS
A geological hammer can be used to break up rocks.

Standard geological hammer

CHISELS
A hammer and chisel are valuable aids when removing fossils from their matrix (the piece of surrounding rock).

Hammer for use with a chisel

TROWELS
Fossils in soft sediment, especially sand, may be removed using a trowel.

GEOLOGICAL MAP
Geological maps are useful for locating promising places to collect fossils, as they help in identifying the age, location, and name of rock formations.

HAND LENS
A pocket hand lens with a magnification of 10 to 20 times is valuable for examining fossils in the field.

BRUSHES
Brushes can be used for brushing away sediment during excavation of fossils from soft rocks.

29

E

Safety helmet

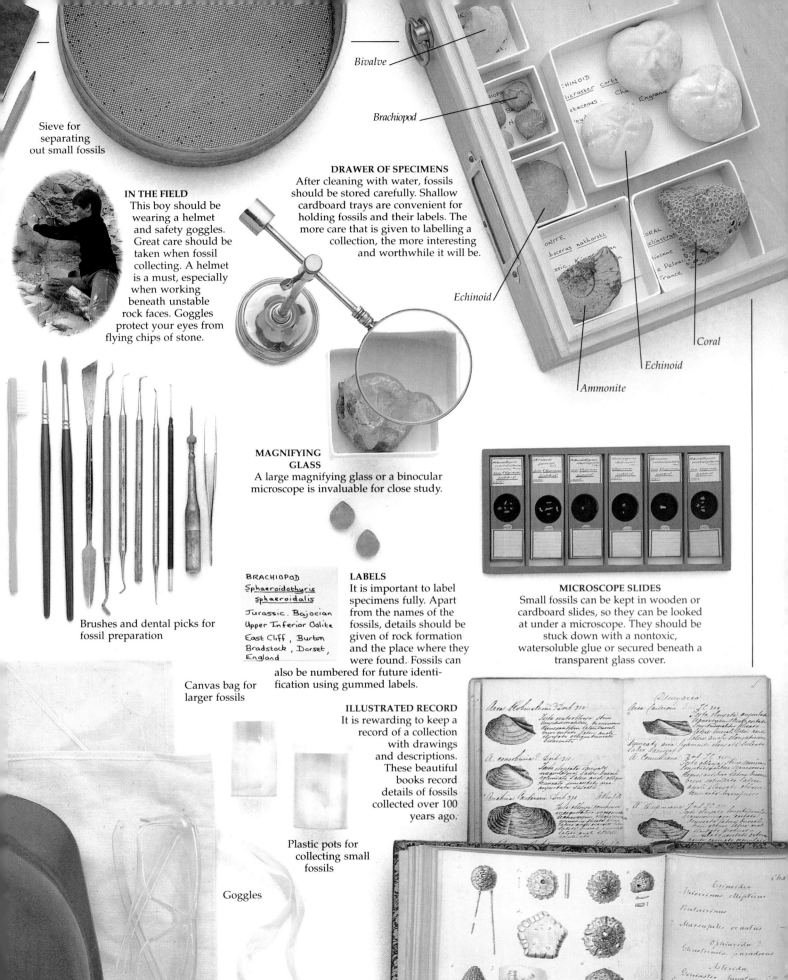

Sieve for separating out small fossils

IN THE FIELD
This boy should be wearing a helmet and safety goggles. Great care should be taken when fossil collecting. A helmet is a must, especially when working beneath unstable rock faces. Goggles protect your eyes from flying chips of stone.

DRAWER OF SPECIMENS
After cleaning with water, fossils should be stored carefully. Shallow cardboard trays are convenient for holding fossils and their labels. The more care that is given to labelling a collection, the more interesting and worthwhile it will be.

Bivalve

Brachiopod

Echinoid

Ammonite

Echinoid

Coral

Brushes and dental picks for fossil preparation

MAGNIFYING GLASS
A large magnifying glass or a binocular microscope is invaluable for close study.

BRACHIOPOD
Sphaeroidothyris sphaeroidalis
Jurassic. Bajocian
Upper Inferior Oolite
East Cliff, Burton
Bradstock, Dorset,
England

LABELS
It is important to label specimens fully. Apart from the names of the fossils, details should be given of rock formation and the place where they were found. Fossils can also be numbered for future identification using gummed labels.

MICROSCOPE SLIDES
Small fossils can be kept in wooden or cardboard slides, so they can be looked at under a microscope. They should be stuck down with a nontoxic, watersoluble glue or secured beneath a transparent glass cover.

Canvas bag for larger fossils

ILLUSTRATED RECORD
It is rewarding to keep a record of a collection with drawings and descriptions. These beautiful books record details of fossils collected over 100 years ago.

Plastic pots for collecting small fossils

Goggles

Did you know?

Dromaeosaur fossil

❀ In the 1990s, paleontologists began to dig up fossils of feathered dinosaurs in China—the best evidence yet that dinosaurs may have evolved into birds. Dromaeosaurs were small, fast-moving meat-eaters that had downy fluff and primitive feathers.

❀ The first fossils of the arthropod *Anomalocaris* were limbs, jaws, or other body parts. No one thought they belonged to one animal. The huge front limbs were thought to be tails from an extinct shrimp. It was only when a complete fossil was found that scientists could picture this strange beast at last.

Record Breakers

❀ **EARLIEST FOSSIL EMBRYO**
The earliest known fossilized animal embryo dates back around 670 million years. It was found in Guizhou province, China.

❀ **OLDEST FOSSIL FLOWER**
A 125-million-year-old flowering plant, named *Archaefructus liaoningensis*, was found in Liaoning province, China, in 1998.

❀ **LARGEST-EVER LAND MAMMAL**
An 83 cm (2 ft 9 in)-long skull fossil found in Mongolia belonged to *Andrewsarchus*, an Eocene carnivore. The entire animal could have been 6 m (19 ft) long and weighed a ton.

❀ **OLDEST FOSSIL FISH**
Two fish, *Haikouichthys ercaicunensis* and *Myllokunmingia fengjiaoa*, were found in rocks from 530 million years ago in Yunnan, China.

❀ **OLDEST FOSSIL MOSS**
The oldest moss fossil is 354 million years old. The moss, *Hepaticites oishii*, was discovered in Yokomichi, Japan, in 1973.

❀ Anomodonts are the most primitive beasts with mammal characteristics that we know of. The 260-million-year-old skull of one was found in South Africa in 1999. About the size of sheep, anomodonts were plant-eaters that lived long before the dinosaurs. They had some reptilian characteristics and some mammalian.

❀ Fossils of an early whale, *Ambulocetus*, show that it was about 10 ft (3 m) long and looked like a big, furry crocodile! Although it had the teeth and skull of a whale and was an excellent swimmer, it also had legs for walking on land. Its name means "walking whale."

❀ At Holzmaden, Germany, there are fossil specimens of thousands of Jurassic marine creatures. One of the most amazing is an ichthyosaur fossilized in the act of giving birth.

Opalized brachiopod

❀ Australia has large opal deposits that formed in the early Cretaceous Period. During mining for opal gems, beautiful specimens of opalized shellfish have been found, especially brachiopods. However, one of the finest opal fossils is "Eric," a complete pliosaur skeleton. Pliosaurs were marine reptiles that lived at the time of the dinosaurs.

Fossilized insect and spider in amber

❀ In the *Jurassic Park* movies, DNA from the bodies of insects fossilized in amber was used to reconstruct whole herds of dinosaurs. Scientists have extracted DNA in this way, but only fragments of it—not enough to rebuild prehistoric animals.

❀ The first complete Pleistocene animal was excavated in 1999 by French paleontologist Bernard Buigues. The Siberian woolly mammoth had lain frozen for over 20,000 years. It was named "Jarkov," after the family of reindeer herders who first discovered it.

❀ In the 1990s, paleontologists found remains of the earliest-known primate: a jawbone and an anklebone the length of a grain of rice. Nicknamed the "Dawn Monkey," *Eosimias* was a mouse-sized primate that lived 40 to 45 million years ago in what is now China.

"Eric," the opalized pliosaur

QUESTIONS AND ANSWERS

Pederpes finneyae

Q Where are the oldest fossils on Earth?

A British Columbia's Burgess Shale used to be the best site for Cambrian fossils, but now older finds are coming out of a series of sites near Kunming, in the province of Yunnan, southwest China. Preserved in rock known as the Maotianshan shales, they include the earliest examples of fish yet discovered. Thousands of near-perfect soft-bodied fossils have been found. Collectively, they are known as the "Chengjiang fauna," after a village near the sites.

Q Where in the world is the Petrified Forest?

A The Petrified Forest is a collection of fossilized logs and tree trunks scattered across an area of national park in the Arizona desert. They date back nearly 220 million years. In addition to plant fossils, there are also some amazing animal finds. These include around 40 fossilized bee nests—the earliest ever found—and lots of bone fragments from vertebrates including dinosaurs, pterosaurs, fish, primitive reptiles, and amphibians such as metoposaurs.

Q Which animal was first to walk on land?

A The earliest fossil evidence is the skeleton of a 3 ft (1 m)-long amphibian, *Pederpes finneyae*, that lived 345 million years ago. All the earlier feet fossils that have been found were designed to point back, and would have been used for swimming. *Pederpes'* ankle joints were evolved to take steps forward. *Pederpes* probably spent some time on land and some in the water. It lived in swamps in what is now Scotland.

Q Where did reptiles turn into mammals?

A Fossil hunters working in the Karoo Basin, South Africa, have found plenty of evidence of various "mammal-like" reptiles, called therapsids. These include the hippopotamus-like *Lystrosaurus*, the saber-toothed predator, *Lycaenops*, and cat-sized *Thrinaxodon*. All of these creatures had characteristics of reptiles, but their teeth were more like those of mammals. This is exciting for scientists. By examining the therapsid fossils they can start to understand the evolutionary changes that led to the first true mammals.

A dig in Yunnan province, China

Q Which American river is stocked full of fossilized fish?

A The world's richest fish fossil site is the Green River Formation at Fossil Butte National Monument, Wyoming, which covers an area of 25,000 sq miles (64,750 sq km). The fossils date back some 55 million years to the Eocene Epoch, when there were a series of large inland lakes on the site. The dead animals and plants that sank to the bottom of these lakes have been exquisitely preserved. Thousands of fish specimens have been found, from at least 20 different genera, including stingrays, catfish, herring, and trout. There are also fossils of turtles, birds, mammals, and crocodiles.

Diplomystus denatus, or herring, from the Green River Formation

Q Which are the oldest human fossils?

A In July 2001, scientists in Ethiopia announced the oldest known traces of human life. Over the previous four years they had discovered fossils belonging to around five specimens of *Ardipithecus ramidus*, a hominid that lived between 5.2 and 5.8 million years ago. These included a jawbone, arm, hand, collar bones, toe bone, and teeth. Just a few months earlier, French scientists announced the discovery of a six-million-year-old creature, *Orrorin tugenensis*, in Kenya. This could be an even earlier human ancestor than *Ardipithecus*, but there is not yet enough evidence to classify it as a hominid.

Fossilized sections of tree trunk in the Petrified Forest, Arizona

Identifying fossils

FOSSILS CAN BE SPLIT INTO THREE GROUPS: plants, and animals with or without backbones. There are also trace fossils, such as animal tracks and coprolites. In each group, the fossil record is vast. If you ever have trouble identifying a fossil find, see if a local museum can help.

FAKE FLOWER
This may look like a flower, but scientists think it was a very primitive animal, not a plant. It lived on the Precambrian seabed and was found in the fossil-rich rocks of the Ediacara Hills, Australia.

FOSSIL ID
This page is from a book that identifies invertebrate fossil finds.

PLANT FOSSILS

TREE TRUNK
Tree trunks withstand the fossilization process well. Whole forests of preserved trunks have been found, with the growth rings visible and intact.

SEQUOIA CONE
The ironstone fossil above is a pine cone from a redwood tree called a sequoia. The oldest sequoia fossils date to Jurassic times—and the trees are still around today.

CLUBMOSS
The clubmoss fossil here is *Archaeosigillaria*, which grew in the Carboniferous Period. At that time, clubmosses grew as tall as trees; today's few species are small plants.

FERN
This fern leaf was found in Hermit shale in the southwestern United States. Shales and mudstones are some of the best places to find fossils of soft plant parts.

ANIMAL FOSSILS: VERTEBRATES

BIRD
One of the world's most famous fossils, this is *Archaeopteryx*, the oldest known bird. Bavarian limestone preserved the fine imprints of its feathers and claws.

REPTILE
This skeleton is of *Pachypleurosaurus*, a reptile that lived in what is now Europe in the Middle Triassic Period. It measured around 47 in (120 cm) long.

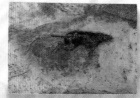

MAMMAL
This fossil of *Macrocranion*, an Eocene hedgehog, was found at Grube Messel, Germany. The shale preserved mammals' soft body parts as well as skeletons.

FISH
This freshwater perch, *Priscacara*, was discovered in the fossil-rich Green River Formation in Wyoming. It dates to the Middle Eocene Epoch.

TEETH
The vertebrate fossils that amateur hunters are most likely to find are teeth. Sharks, in particular, shed many teeth over a lifetime.

ANIMAL FOSSILS: INVERTEBRATES

BELEMNITE
Belemnites were mollusks related to modern-day squid and octopus. After fossilization, all that is left is the animal's inside shell, or guard.

TRILOBITE
Encrinurus, fossilized here in limestone, lived in shallow seas in the Silurian Period. Its distinctive head shield has earned it the nickname "strawberry-headed trilobite."

CRINOID (SEA-LILY)
Crinoids were common in the Paleozoic seas. This one is *Cupressocrinites*, found in Germany. Its petal-like arms would have filtered food from the sea water.

BRACHIOPOD
About 0.75 in (2 cm) long, this brachiopod is *Goniorhynchia*, which lived in the Middle Jurassic Period. It was found in a layer of forest marble in England.

AMMONITE
Gunnarites is a Late Cretaceous ammonite with a very distinctive shell. On this gray sandstone fossil, a tiny fragment of the original shell can still be seen, top left.

FORAMINIFERAN (MICROFOSSIL)
This highly-magnified image shows the fossilized test of *Elphidium*. This single-celled protozoa is tiny—about the size of the head of a pin.

BIVALVE
Around 2.75 in (7 cm) long, this Jurassic oyster would have cemented itself to a rock on the seabed. Called *Gryphaea*, its popular name is the Devil's toenail.

CORAL
Colpophyllia is often called "brain coral", because of the distinctive shape formed by the colony. This fossil, found in Italy, dates to the Late Oligocene Epoch.

GASTROPOD
This snail is *Pleurotomaria*, or slit shell. It has distinctive, nobbly riblets on the shoulders of the whorls. A living relative is pictured on page 61.

SPONGE
This Early Cretaceous sponge, *Raphidonema farringdonense*, is about 3.25 in (8 cm) high. It was common in warm, shallow seas in what is now Oxfordshire, England.

GRAPTOLITE
These are *Rhabdinopora*, the earliest graptolite plankton. Graptolite fossils show not one animal but a colony of creatures that floated on the surface of the sea.

ECHINOID (SEA URCHIN)
This extinct urchin, *Phymosoma*, lived on the sea floor in the Late Cretaceous Period. Its test and its many spines have been fossilized in chalk.

Find out more

THERE ARE SO MANY WAYS that you can find out more about fossils. Go to visit local or national museums and you will see some spectacular collections. You could look out for television programs about fossil hunters and their exciting new finds. Visit a library or fossil Web sites to read up more on the subject. You could also become a fossil hunter. To do this safely, it is a good idea to join a local club, if there is one in your area. You can benefit from the guidance and expertise of the club leader. Fossil collecting is great fun, and you will soon build up your own collection to display.

PALEONTOLOGISTS IN THE LAB
At this French laboratory, experts are carefully removing fossilized bones from a plaster cast. The plaster was set around the fossils at the place they were discovered to protect them from damage during transportation. Casts are also taken of precious, fragile fossils for displaying. Many of the fossils on show in museums are casts.

AMATEUR FOSSIL HUNTER
It takes a great deal of patience to be a fossil hunter. You might often come home empty-handed, so it is important to enjoy the quest for its own sake. This fossil hunter in Florida is sifting through shingle, a method suitable only for certain beaches.

JET NECKLACE
See how many "fossils" you can find in a day. Amber and jet are really just fossilized plant matter. Think about fossil fuels, too, such as coal and oil, and their many by-products.

PALEONTOLOGIST AT WORK
Dinosaur National Monument, Colorado, is a protected site. Its fossilized dinosaur bones are exposed or dug out by professionals who will not damage them. If you are interested in a career as a paleontologist, focus on science studies and try to gather lots of experience on organized digs.

USEFUL WEBSITES

- The American Museum of Natural History's site includes games and activities along with informative interviews with dinosaurs and paleontologists. **ology.amnh.org/paleontology/**

- The San Diego Natural History Museum shows kids how to find fossils—in museums or their own backyards: **www.sdnhm.org/kids/dinosaur/**

- From the Royal Ontario Museum, learn about who studies fossils and why: **www.rom.on.ca/quiz/fossil/**

- Visit links to natural history museums around the world **www.ucmp.berkeley.edu/subway/nathistmus.html**

AMERICAN MUSEUM OF NATURAL HISTORY, NEW YORK, NEW YORK
Home to the world's largest collection of vertebrate fossils, 600 of which are on view. Highlights include:
• *Buettneria*, an early four-limbed animal
• *Pteranodon* fossil
• new reconstructions of *T-rex* and *Apatosaurus*.

PAGE MUSEUM, LA BREA TAR PITS, LOS ANGELES, CALIFORNIA
Home to the largest and most diverse collection of Ice Age plant and animal fossils in the world. Visitors can see:
• scientists restore, examine, and clean fossils still being found in the tar pits
• Hancock Park, home to more than 100 tar pits where scientists continue to find fossils.

PETRIFIED FOREST NATIONAL PARK, ARIZONA
The largest and most beautifully preserved natural concentration of petrified wood in the world. Attractions include:
• fossilized trees more than 200 million years old
• fossils—some of the oldest known to man—found in the park.

NATIONAL MUSEUM OF NATURAL HISTORY, WASHINGTON, D.C.
Part of the Smithsonian Institution, this museum has the world's biggest collection of Burgess Shale fauna, as well as:
• 40 dinosaurs on display
• a collection of more than 200,000 foraminifera.

UNDER THE MICROSCOPE
At Earthlab in London's Natural History Museum, visitors can handle real specimens and examine them under a microscope. There are experts on hand to answer questions and to help visitors identify fossils they have found. The inner gallery also has a useful library of reference material.

THE CAMBRIDGE MUSEUM
Founded in 1814, the University Museum of Zoology in Cambridge, England, houses a superb collection of fossils. It includes fish from Canada and Scotland, mammals from North America, and reptiles from Africa. The permanent display aims to show one example of every animal—living or extinct—using fossils and stuffed specimens.

DINOSAUR MUSEUM
Europe's first museum dedicated solely to dinosaurs opened at Espéraza in southern France in 1992. Many of its display items are fossils dug from Late Cretaceous rock deposits nearby. As well as bones, the collection includes eggs, like those of the titanosaur above, and casts of fossilized footprints.

THE NATURAL HISTORY MUSEUM, PARIS
The entomology gallery in France's Natural History Museum has some of the oldest fossilized insects on Earth. There is also a paleobotany department dedicated to plant fossils and a gallery of evolution with many fossil skeletons and casts.

Glossary

Anthracite

AMBER Fossilized resin of an ancient conifer

AMMONITE An extinct cephalopod with a shell, common in the Mesozoic era

AMPHIBIAN A cold-blooded, slimy-skinned animal adapted to life on land and in water

ANATOMIST Someone who studies the structure of animals

ANGIOSPERM A flowering plant that protects its seeds inside a fruit

ANTHRACITE Hard, shiny, jet-black coal

ARTHROPOD An animal with jointed legs, a segmented body, and an exoskeleton, such as a trilobite

BACTERIUM One of the simplest living organisms

BELEMNITE Extinct cephalopod related to the modern-day squid

BIVALVE An animal with two similar shells, such as a cockle

BRACHIOPOD An animal with two shells, one slightly larger than the other

Eocene angiosperm

BYSSAL THREAD One of the stringlike attachments that fix a bivalve to the rocks

CAMBRIAN The geological period that lasted from 545 to 495 mya

CARBONIFEROUS The geological period that lasted from 354 to 290 mya

CARNIVORE An animal from the *Carnivora* group

CENOZOIC Our present geological era, which began 65 mya; the age of mammals

CEPHALOPOD A mollusk with tentacles

CLIMATE The average weather of a place over a period of time

Diplomystus, or herring, from the Early Eocene

COPROLITE Fossilized animal dropping

CORAL A build-up of polyps' skeletons, that may grow into a reef

CRETACEOUS The last geological period of the Mesozoic; lasted from 142 to 65 mya

CREVASSE A deep crack in a glacier

CRINOID Primitive echinoderm with a cupped body and branching arms

CRUST The thin outer layer of the Earth. It varies in thickness between 4.33 and 43.5 miles (7 and 70 km) thick.

CRUSTACEAN An arthropod with a hard shell, jointed legs, and compound eyes

DENDRITE A crystal that forms branches

DEVONIAN The geological period that lasted from 417 to 354 mya

Devonian fish

ECHINODERM A marine animal with five-point symmetry, for example, a starfish

ELEMENT Material that cannot be broken down into more simple substances by chemical means

EOCENE The geological epoch that lasted from 55 to 34 mya, when mammals became the dominant land vertebrates

EROSION The wearing away of rock by wind, water, and ice

EVOLUTION The process by which species change into new ones over millions of generations; it happens as some characteristics are kept and others are lost

EXOSKELETON Tough outer casing that protects the body of some invertebrates

EXTINCT Describes an animal or plant that has died out

FOSSIL The naturally preserved remains of animals or plants, or evidence of them

FOSSIL FUEL Materials formed from the remains of ancient living things that can be burned to give off energy—for example, oil

GEOLOGY The study of rocks

GLACIER A slow-moving river of ice

GYMNOSPERM A plant that produces and protects its seeds in a cone

HERBIVORE Grazing or browsing animal

HOLOCENE Our present geological epoch, which began 10,000 years ago, when humans became the dominant land vertebrates

HOMINID A member of the family *Hominidae*, which includes extinct and modern humans

ICTHYOSAUR An extinct, dolphin-like marine reptile that lived in the Mesozoic

IGNEOUS ROCK Rock formed as magma cooled and hardened in the Earth's crust

IMPERVIOUS Describes rock that liquid cannot penetrate

INVERTEBRATE An animal without a backbone, such as a shellfish or insect

JURASSIC The geological period that lasted from 206 to 142 mya

LIMESTONE A sedimentary rock made of the fossilized remains of ancient creatures

LYCOPOD The clubmosses, a group of primitive plants that reproduce by spores

MAGMA Molten rock beneath the Earth's surface

MAMMAL A warm-blooded, hair-covered animal that usually gives birth to live young

MESOZOIC The geological era that lasted from 248 to 65 mya, also known as the age of the dinosaurs

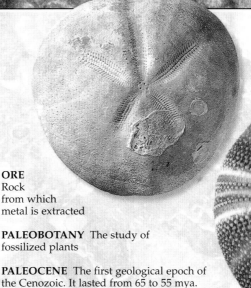

The tests (skeletons) of a fossilized sand dollar, left, and a modern sea urchin, below

ORE Rock from which metal is extracted

PALEOBOTANY The study of fossilized plants

PALEOCENE The first geological epoch of the Cenozoic. It lasted from 65 to 55 mya.

PALEONTOLOGY The study of fossils

PALEOZOIC The geological era that lasted from 545 to 248 mya, when land plants developed and the dominant animals were fish and marine invertebrates

PANGAEA Supercontinent that formed in the Late Paleozoic and began to break up in the Mesozoic

PERMIAN The last geological period of the Paleozoic; lasted from 290 to 248 mya

PIGMENT The chemicals that give something its coloring

PLACODERM An extinct fish with armor and jaws that lived from the Late Silurian to the Early Carboniferous

PLEISTOCENE The geological epoch that lasted from two million to 10,000 ya, the time of the last Ice Age

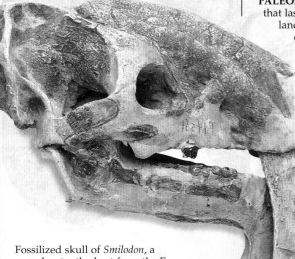

Fossilized skull of *Smilodon*, a saber-toothed cat from the Eocene

METAMORPHIC ROCK Rock that forms due to the action of heat and pressure, or heat alone

MINERAL A solid mixture of chemicals that has certain regular characteristics, such as atomic structure. The name relates to mining.

MIOCENE The geological epoch that lasted from 24 to 5 mya

MOLLUSK An invertebrate that is unsegmented

NATURALIST Someone who studies nature, especially animals or plants

NODULE A rounded lump of hard rock

OLIGOCENE The geological epoch that lasted from 34 to 24 mya

OPAL A gem composed of hydrous silica

ORDOVICIAN The geological period that lasted from 495 to 443 mya

PLESIOSAUR An extinct, long-necked marine reptile that lived in the Mesozoic

PLIOCENE The geological epoch that lasted from five to two mya

POLYP A tiny marine invertebrate. Whole colonies of polyps form corals and reefs.

PRECAMBRIAN The earliest geological period, which lasted from 4,600 mya, when Earth formed, until 545 mya

PTEROSAUR An extinct flying reptile that lived in the Mesozoic

REPTILE A cold-blooded, scaly animal that usually reproduces by laying eggs

RESOURCE A useful material. Natural resources include wood, oil, and iron.

ROCK Solid mixtures, or aggregates, of minerals

SEDIMENTARY ROCK Rock that forms at the Earth's surface. It is made of layers of rock fragments and other substances such as mud that have been deposited on top of each other.

SHALE A rock made of compacted clay

SILURIAN The geological period that lasted from 443 to 417 mya.

STRATIFICATION The formation of layers, or bands, of rock

TEST An echinoid's plated skeleton

TRACE FOSSIL Fossilized evidence of the activities of an animal, such as burrows, footprints, or coprolites

TRIASSIC The first geological period of the Mesozoic; lasted from 248 to 206 mya

VERTEBRATE An animal with a backbone, such as a fish, frog, or human being

A sea sponge from the Cretaceous

Index

Acknowledgments

The publisher would like to thank:
Plymouth Marine Laboratory, National Museum of Wales, Kew Gardens for specimens for photography; Lester Cheeseman and Thomas Keenes for additional design assistance; Anna Kunst for editorial assistance; Meryl Silbert; Karl Shone for additional photography (pp. 18–19); Jane Parker for the index

The author would like to thank:
M.K. Howarth; C Patterson; R.A. Fortey; C.H.C. Brunton; A.W. Gentry; B.R. Rosen; J.B. Richardson; P.L. Forey; N.J. Morris; C.B. Stringer; A.B. Smith; J.E.P. Whittaker; R. Croucher; S.F. Morris; C.R. Hill; A.C. Milner; R.L. Hodgkinson; C.A. Walker; R.J. Cleevely; C.H. Shute; V.T. Young; D.N. Lewis; A.E. Longbottom; M. Crawley; R. Kruszynski; C. Bell; S.C. Naylor; A. Lum; R.W. Ingle; P.D. Jenkins; P.D. Hillyard; D.T. Moore; J.W. Schopf; C.M. Butler; P.W. Jackson

Picture Credits
t=top, b=bottom, m=middle, l=left, r=right

Aldus Archive: 53tm, 54bl;
Alison Anholt-White: 28tl;
Ardea: 9bl, 21m, 42m, 42bl, 43t, 61tm;
Biofotos/Heather Angel: 26m, 31mr, 39br, 44–5bm, 60tr;
Booth Museum of Natural History 66bl;
Bridgeman Art Library: 14mr; /Musée Cluny/Lauros-Giraudon 17tl;
Dept. of Earth Sciences, University of Cambridge: 39mr;
Cleveland Museum of Natural History, Ohio: 59m;
Bruce Coleman: 8br, 22m; /Jeff Foote 28tr, 39m, 40m; /Fritz Prenzel 57br; /Kim Campbell 59ml;
Simon Conway Morris: 20m;

Corbis: James L. Amos 65br, 68bl;
Mary Evans Picture Library: 13ml, 14br, 15tl, 20m, 48t, 52tl, 54t, 54br, 55t, 55mr, 55b, 62m;
Vivien Fifield: 50bl;
Geological Society: 46t;
Geoscience Features Picture Library: 9tr, 51tl, 51tm, 51tr;
David George: 25m;
Robert Harding Picture Library: 21br, 29m, 59b;
Michael Holford: 12tl;
Hunterian Museum: 66tl;
Hutchison Library: 24tl, 57mr;
Mansell Collection: 26t, 40b;
Natural History Museum, London: 66tr, 70m, 66tm, 66ml, 66bm (below), 69t; /Geological Museum of China 64tl;
Oxford Scientific Films: 44bl, 53bm;
Oxford University Museum: 66br (above), 71tm, 71b;
Planet Earth Pictures: 32ml, 41m,

43ml, 44mr, 63tl;
Rex Features: Sipa Press 65m;
Ann Ronan Picture Library: 15tm, 50br;
Royal Tyrell Museum, Canada: 66bm (above);
Science Photo Library: 58r; /Tony Craddock 65bl; /Peter Menzel 64b; /Philippe Plailly 68t; /Philippe Plailly/Eurelios 69ml, 69mr; /Andrew Syred 67mr (above)
Paul Taylor: 19b;
University Museum of Zoology, Cambridge: 69b; /Sarah Finney (GLAHM 100815) 65t;
ZEFA: 20–21bl
Jacket images: Front: Sinclair Stammers/Science Photo Library, b; James L Amos/Corbis, tr
Illustrations by: John Woodcock, Eugene Fleury
Original picture research by: Kathy Lockley